Ashes To Ascension

*Second Lesson Sermons
For Lent/Easter
Cycle B*

John A. Stroman

CSS Publishing Company, Inc., Lima, Ohio

ASHES TO ASCENSION

Copyright © 1999 by
CSS Publishing Company, Inc.
Lima, Ohio

Scripture quotations unless otherwise marked are from the *New Revised Standard Version of the Bible*, copyright 1989 by the Division of Christian Education of the National Council of the Churches of Christ in the USA. Used by permission.

Scripture quotations marked NEB are from *The New English Bible*. Copyright © the Delegates of the Oxford University Press and the Syndics of the Cambridge University Press, 1961, 1970. Reprinted by permission.

Library of Congress Cataloging-in-Publication Data

Stroman, John A.
    Ashes to Ascension : second lesson sermons for Lent/Easter : cycle B / John A. Stroman.
      p.   cm.
    ISBN 0-7880-1509-5 (pbk. : alk. paper)
    1. Lenten sermons. 2. Holy-Week sermons. 3 Easter Sermons. 4. Bible. N.T. Epistles Sermons. 5. Methodist Church Sermons. 6. Sermons, American. I. Title.
BV4277.S85   1999
252'.62—dc21   99-16009
                                                                             CIP

This book is available in the following formats, listed by ISBN:
    0-7880-1509-5   Book
    0-7880-1510-9   Disk
    0-7880-1511-7   Sermon Prep

For more information about CSS Publishing Company resources, visit our website at www.csspub.com.

PRINTED IN U.S.A.

*To the faculty and students
at Trinity Theological College,
Legon, Ghana, West Africa,
who taught me the meaning
of Christian love and commitment.*

Table Of Contents

Introduction

During the academic year of 1997-98 I was a visiting lecturer in New Testament at Trinity Theological College in Ghana, West Africa. It was during this time that a portion of this work was completed. The students in my class along with laity and clergy in the Methodist Church in Ghana, for whom I have such great respect and appreciation, provided me with both inspiration and insight.

Beginning with Ash Wednesday the preacher and people embark on a very important pilgrimage together that goes through the weeks of Lent, reaching its moment of triumph on Easter Sunday. The Lenten season is a special period that provides the preacher with texts and themes that represent the deepest concerns of those who come to worship. These epistle texts deal with the ministry of reconciliation, suffering, and the meaning of the cross within the Christian life, ending with the theme of grace — the unmerited, undeserved, unearned goodness of God extended to all of us through Jesus Christ.

The Eastertide texts are from 1 John. In our world of violence and anger here are timely texts that make it possible for the preacher to connect with his or her people at the point of their greatest need. The theme of love in 1 John, a love for God and for one another, is timely. This is a message for our time that merits proclamation. There is no doubt that 1 John through the centuries has enriched souls, kindled faith, and inspired love. Here is a word that needs to be heard.

John A. Stroman
Trinity Theological College
Legon, Ghana
West Africa

Beginning The Journey To Calvary

2 Corinthians 5:20b—6:10

For centuries Christians have gathered on Ash Wednesday to begin the Lenten journey to Calvary. The palm branches from the previous Palm/Passion Sunday are burnt, providing the ashes for the service. The form and content of this special service have always focused on the dual themes of sin and death in light of God's redeeming love in Jesus Christ. The imposition of the ashes seems appropriate with their dark earth color, somber hue, and rough texture suggesting the character of the day and the Lenten journey that lies ahead. Worshipers kneeling at the altar rail receive the ashes in the form of a cross on their foreheads. Through the centuries this has been a powerful, nonverbal, experiential way of participating in the call to repentance and reconciliation. It is a time to think on what it means to be reconciled by God and to reflect on the apostle's words, "in Christ God was reconciling the world to himself" (v. 19a), and "God ... has given us the ministry of reconciliation" (v. 18b).

The Possibility Of Reconciliation
The apostle challenges the Corinthians "to be reconciled to God." He is saying that before you can ever enter this "ministry of reconciliation" you must be reconciled. Before you can witness to grace, you must experience grace. Before you begin to talk about deliverance, you need to experience deliverance. His initial point is, "Be reconciled to God." The apostle points out that this reconciliation with God is possible because through Christ, God has taken the initiative. The apostle Paul states this clearly in two passages:

9

"We were reconciled to God through the death of his son" (Romans 5:10), and "... reconciling both groups to God in one body through the cross" (Ephesisans 2:16).

How is this reconciliation possible? His answer is stated in verse 21: "For our sake he made him sin who knew no sin, so that in him we might become the righteousness of God." This verse sets forth the gospel of reconciliation in all of its mystery and wonder. "There is no sentence more profound in the whole of Scripture; for this verse embraces the whole ground of the sinner's reconciliation to God" (Philip Hughes, *New International Commentary*, 2 Corinthians, p. 211). The phrase in verse 21, "So that in him we might become the righteousness of God," is essential. "On him" the full force of God's judgment against sin has fallen. So that "in him" the sinner finds shelter from that judgment. It is "in him" that the sinner is made the righteousness of God. Listen to the words of Isaiah 53:5-6: "But he was wounded for our transgressions, crushed for our iniquities; upon him was the punishment that made us whole, and by his bruises we are healed ... and the Lord laid on him the iniquity of us all." Our sins are transferred to him and his righteousness is transferred to us.

Yet, we must not lose sight of the freedom of Christ's action. The Son is not the unwilling victim of the Father's wrath. The freedom of Christ's actions and the harmony of the mind and purpose which he enjoyed with the Father are clearly conveyed in the words of John 10:17-18: "For this reason the Father loves me, because I lay down my life in order to take it up again. No one takes it from me, but I lay it down of my own accord. I have power to lay it down, and I have the power to take it up again ... " Later the apostle writes, "But he (Christ) emptied himself, taking the form of a slave, being born in human likeness. And being found in human form, he humbled himself and became obedient to the point of death — even death on a cross" (Philippians 2:7-8). The fact is that reconciliation is achieved through the death of Christ and reconciliation cannot be severed from atonement.

Therefore, reconciliation with God and with one another is possible because of the death and resurrection of Jesus Christ. In Romans Paul reminds us: "But now in Christ Jesus you who once were far off have been brought near by the blood of Christ. For he is our peace; in his flesh he has made both groups into one and has broken down the dividing wall, that is, the hostility between us ... no longer strangers and aliens ... but citizens ... saints ... members of the household of God" (Ephesians 2:13-14, 19).

Paul has not forgotten the burden of his own ministry and its theme of reconciliation. This theme is *autobiographical* for him. When he speaks about walls of hostility being removed, he is reflecting on his own life regarding the hostility that he had felt toward the Christian community. He knows the meaning of being reconciled and having walls and barriers removed. Thus, he can speak confidently about the possibilities of reconciliation for all of us.

Called To The Ministry Of Reconciliation

Paul cannot forget the main theme of his ministry — reconciliation. He reminds all who would be followers of Christ that Christ also "has given us this ministry of reconciliation" (5:18b). Today we begin our pilgrimage to Calvary, and as we think about the life of Christ and his ministry, now is the time for us to think about our ministry. Paul reminds us that all who are called to minister in Christ's name are called to the ministry of reconciliation.

What does it mean to have a ministry of reconciliation? It means to be used by God as the instruments of God's love and grace within the world. It means to bring together the enemies of God and make them the friends of God. It means to help reunite broken relationships between men and women and with one another. It means that you will see to it that your life and your witness will help to tear down barriers that divide, separate, and alienate, establishing peace and harmony. It means that the goal of your life will be given to the establishing of lasting relationships of love and bringing an end to hostilities.

The apostle reminds us that this is the minstry that God has given to us and "God is making his appeal through us" (5:20). Recall the words of Stradivari, the maker of violins, as George Eliot interprets him:

... for while God gives the violinist skill
I give them instruments to play upon.
God choosing me to help him
... God could not make
Antonio Stradivari's violins
without Antonio!

The fact remains that God has chosen people like you and me to be his ambassadors and representatives. God has always done it that way — that has been God's method. When God sought a people to reveal his purpose to the world, he chose Abraham to be the father of that people. When God sought to lead the people from the slavery of Egypt, Moses became the man of the hour. When God needed a voice to speak out against moral decadence, God chose Amos, the simple shepherd from Tokoa, to carry the message. When God sought to move into human life and activity, God's plan and purpose was entrusted to a young struggling carpenter and his teenage wife amid the obscurity and poverty of the Judean hills. If the work of reconciliation is to be done in our day, it will be because someone somewhere has heard God's call and responded in obedience and faith. Have you ever considered how every advance in human relations, every human triumph in justice and freedom, every forward step in science, every discovery that provides a breakthrough in science and medicine is the result of men and women cooperating with God?

At the time when the Berlin Wall was about to be torn down the *National Geographic* magazine had a two-page spread of an aerial photograph of the entire Berlin Wall. It showed clearly the two walls that had been built, and between them was a no-man's-land filled with all kinds of debris of destruction, such as upturned spikes, barbed wire, electric fences, trip alarms, watchdogs, floodlights, and vehicle traps. To my surprise I saw in the middle of all these objects of hostility and division an abandoned church. Remarkably, it was called the Church of Reconciliation. What a powerful symbol of what the Church is and what the Church could be. Today, that is where the Church finds itself, right in the midst of a hostile and divided world seeking to carry out Christ's ministry of reconciliation.

A Reconciling Ministry Beyond The Church

Our ministry of reconciliation takes us far beyond the walls of our sanctuaries. There is a tendency and temptation for the Church today to fall back into the trap of the medieval Church, who considered that what was being done within the church was more important than what was being done in the world. This heresy has always plagued the church. The church is not to be the object of its own mission. God help us if we spend all of our time, energy, and money on ourselves. Recent studies of church life have revealed that churches which are primarily concerned with their own existing members' needs are unlikely to grow. As the body of Christ, the Church gathers together so that it may disperse. The Church comes to worship so that it may leave to serve. The Church comes to pray and speak with God, so it may leave and speak to others in God's name. The Church comes to strengthen its life together in worship, prayer, word, and sacrament so that it may leave and give its life for others.

Today is Ash Wednesday, the first day of Lent. It is a time for us to reflect on the life and teachings of Jesus and his ministry and what all of this means for our own Christian lives. It is a time to consider how we, through Christ, can gain a greater understanding of how we can become God's agents of love and reconciliation in a broken and divided world. It is a time for us to see if we are contributing more to our community's and world's problems and hostility than being part of its healing and wholeness. It is time for us to take seriously God's call to the ministry of reconciliation and to realize that what we have to offer in this ministry to others is not our intelligence, skill, power, influence, or connections but our own human brokenness through which the love of God can manifest itself. There is no greater ministry than this.

13

Once And For All

1 Peter 3:18-22

We approach this first Sunday of Lent with mixed feelings. Normally we come to church because we want to sing and celebrate and we trust that the mood will make us feel good about ourselves. On this first Sunday of Lent things are different. The mood is more somber, prayers are penitential, and there is talk of confession and repentance. Such things as sacrifices and self-denial are suggested. The penitential acts of honesty reiterate, despite our intentions, achievements, and appearances, that we are sinful. In other words: we sin.

Sin is not something that many people have spent much time talking about or worrying about through the years of the cultural and sexual revolution. We have done a good job developing subtle, elaborate mechanisms in the defense and denial of sin. Jung said, "The darker the shadow inside, the more polished the mask we must wear." There is a cost to a life that is spent polishing the mask. Will Willimon points out that the Christian faith has an odd response to all of this, "You can repent." Christ gives us the resources to be honest about ourselves. We don't have to polish the mask, for Christ sees the shadow we're attempting to hide beneath. Christ knows all about our sinful past, and he makes it his own. Christ's strong love for us, that embraces us and dies for us, enables us to tell the truth.

How appropriate that 1 Peter 3:18-22 should be our text for this first Sunday in Lent. There are many things regarding this text which are difficult and perplexing. Scholars have been haggling over this text for centuries. As one scholar stated, they have examined, probed, dissected, allegorized, and argued about it since the time of Augustine. Ironically, the main theme of the text has not been the main interest of the scholars. Most of the discussion has centered around Jesus' mission to the "spirits in prison." There has been much debate regarding the meaning of "death in the flesh ... alive in the spirit," and of the section, "he went and made a proclamation to the spirits in prison." There has been a great deal of debate about who these imprisoned spirits actually are. The argument has ranged from the spirit of those who disregarded Noah's warning in Genesis 6 regarding the pending flood to "evil angels" where Christ preached to the underworld to disobedient fallen angels. Some have suggested that his journey to the underworld took place in the interim period between Christ's death and resurrection. Others have insisted that this "spiritually alive" Christ is the resurrected Christ and that it took place after the resurrection and prior to the ascension.

Much of this debate is speculation. We need to be careful not to allow what appears to be an endless debate to distort or overshadow the rest of the message in 1 Peter. I agree with Leonard Sweet's statement that "this text provides one of the Bible's most vivid witnesses to the saving power of Christ's sacrifice and his enduring, unceasing love." Emphatically, Paul declares that it is "once for all," pointing out that this single act of the sacrifice of Christ upon the cross is to be distinguished from the repeated deaths of victims under the Levitical system. Those sacrifices needed to be repeated, but the sacrifice of Christ on the cross is "once for all."

Christ Suffered For Our Sins

This text makes a forceful statement on this first Sunday of Lent — Christ suffered for our sins once and for all. This places the death of Christ on the cross at the center of our attention and thinking during this Lenten season. Pheme Perkins has pointed out that Jesus did not die as a heroic leader of a populist movement. Jesus was not crushed by the powerful Roman authorities as a martyr victim. She points out that this may be a popular vision of the cross today, but the New Testament writers do not describe Jesus as a heroic leader of a resistance movement or as a shattered victim of evil. Rather, the New Testament writers insist that the cross depicts God's love for a sinful and undeserving humanity (*The Living Pulpit*, July 1992, p. 16). This is exactly how Paul has described the situation in our text: "For Christ has suffered for sins, once for all, the righteous for the unrighteous...."

This passage also helps us to understand something of the innocent sufferer. Jesus has brought us to God through this shining example of his obedience to the will of God. Jesus endured human suffering with patience and trust to bring us to God. We who were lost without hope are brought to God, as Paul states, being "made nigh by the blood of Christ" (Ephesians 2:13). Those who suffer innocently or seemingly without cause or reason, in the midst of their bitter experience, can obtain a measure of comfort and hope with the promise of Christ's companionship and the inspiration of his example. The real and meaningful way of dealing with human suffering is to view such suffering in light of the suffering of Christ. His suffering provides us with some understanding of our suffering. Christ's suffering can help us to accept our suffering and turn it into a means of grace. Thus, not only do we as lost sinners look to the cross of Jesus as our only hope of being reconciled with God and with one another, but also within Christ's suffering we gain some insight regarding human suffering.

People With A Past

This first Sunday of Lent we need to discover that we are a people with a past. Willimon states: "I expect that a psychiatrist might say that our elaborate defenses and denial of sin are themselves evidences for sin's stark reality. I would have no need to look good in my charitable giving, be seen by others in church, defend my victimization, and fiercely assert my innocence if I did not know, down deep, my sin" (*Pulpit Resources,* January 1997, p. 27). Regardless of your past, our text today points to some very notorious sinners and uses them as examples of how far the scope of God's love in Christ extends. If the comforting and forgiving presence of Christ is able to reach to the prison that held some of history's most disobedient spirits, then surely Christ's saving power and healing presence is available to all today.

Lent reminds us that the sinfulness and sordidness that permeate the world around us percolate in our own hearts. But Lent also reminds us Christ comes to set us free from the burdens and sins of the past by discovering the unconditional nature of God's love for us, forgiving us — setting the captives free.

> *I know not how Calvary's cross*
> *A world from sin could free;*
> *I only know its matchless love*
> *Has brought Christ's love to me.*
> — Henry W. Farrington

The Righteous For The Unrighteous

The apostle reminds us in Romans 5:6 that "Christ died for the ungodly." He goes on to state that rarely would anyone die for a righteous person, but "while we were yet sinners Christ died for us" (5:8b). Love can go no further than that. It is understandable how a person would be willing to die for a noble cause or lay down one's life for a friend. The remarkable thing about Christ is that he laid down his life for us while we were yet sinners. For a people who had no thought of God, no care for God or God's cause. In fact, a people who were sinners and for the most part hostile to God. The fact is, the righteous Jesus laid down his life for the unrighteous so that he may be able "to bring you to God." James D. G. Dunn points out that "God shows his love by doing for man and woman, at the time of need and in the sacrifice of Christ, what they could not do for themselves" (*World Bible Commentary*, vol. 38, p. 267). The apostle is quite clear that the whole saving process, the righteous for the unrighteous, is the proof of God's love. Christ suffered to establish "once for all" that God is love.

We come on this first Sunday of Lent in our fallen state, broken state, confused state, or whatever state we happen to be in. It is good to know regardless of whatever state we find ourselves, because of the suffering love of Christ, the righteous for the unrighteous, we can come to God knowing that we are both loved and accepted just as we are.

18

Mary Ann Bird is a short story writer. She wrote a short story about her own life titled "The Whispering Test." She said she grew up knowing that she was different and she hated it. She told how she was born with a cleft palate, and when she started school her classmates made it clear to her how she looked to others. She was a little girl with a misshapen lip, crooked nose, lopsided teeth, and garbled speech. When schoolmates would ask, "What happened to your lip?" she would tell them that she had fallen and cut it on a piece of glass. She said, "Somehow it seemed more acceptable to have suffered an accident than to have been born different. I was convinced that no one outside of my family could love me." There was a teacher in the second grade whom she adored. Mrs. Leonard was a short, round, happy, and sparkling lady. Annually in her class she would conduct a hearing test which she gave to every student. Students would go to the wall and cover one ear and listen for her to whisper a sentence, and the student would have to repeat it back to her. The teacher would say such sentences as, "The sky is blue," or "Do you have new shoes?" Mary Ann said she went to the far wall and waited for those words that God must have put in her teacher's mouth. Mrs. Leonard whispered to her, "I wish you were my little girl." She said that those seven words changed her life.

You do not need to worry whether you are acceptable to God or not. Regardless of what, who, where you are — God has already made that choice.

Promises
— Promises

Romans 4:13-25

In Romans 4, the apostle turns his attention to Abraham, and rightly so for obvious reasons. As Paul states, "Abraham, our ancestor according to the flesh" (4:1). Abraham is the first and the highly regarded father of the Israelite nation. Abraham was the "friend of God" and to him the founding promises of the nation had been given. James D. G. Dunn points out that "within the Judaism of Paul's day Abraham had long been lauded as, in effect, the prototype of the devoted Jew — that is, one who demonstrated his faithfulness to the Lord under testing, as one who 'in testing was found faithful.' In other words, it looks as though Paul is about to meet head-on a widely current view of Abraham's faith as his *covenant faithfulness* — his loyalty to God and obedience to God's command even under extreme provocation" (Dunn, *Romans*, p. 226).

Beginning with our text in verse 13 Paul is now focusing on the word "promise" in light of the life of Abraham. The apostle is here reiterating Genesis 15:6 as he speaks about a righteousness that was reckoned to Abraham by virtue of his believing the promise of God. It was not through the law that the promise was given Abraham but through the righteousness of faith. Paul is emphatic that God's promise to Abraham did not come to him because he achieved any merit by keeping the law; it was not the result of anything that he had done. It was the result of God's generous grace in answer to Abraham's absolute faith. "The promise, as Paul saw it, was dependant on two things and two things only —

the free grace of God and the perfect faith of Abraham" (Barclay, *Romans,* p. 65).

Paul was very much aware of what had happened to the promise by those who sought to keep it merely by means of the law. Barclay rightly points out that they had completely destroyed the promise, because no person can fully keep the law. "If the promise depends on keeping the law, the promise can never be fulfilled" (Barclay, *Romans,* p. 66). The weakness of the law is that it can diagnose the trouble but cannot effect a cure. The law can point out how a person has gone wrong, but it is powerless to help a person from going wrong. So this is a crucial point for Paul — Abraham did not receive the promise of God because he kept the law, but through his faith and the generosity of God's grace, he received the promise. "The essence of Abraham's faith in this case was that he believed that God could make the impossible possible" (Barclay, *Romans,* p. 69).

Struggling With God's Promise

Through Abraham's faith and God's grace Abraham received the promise, but not without a struggle. After Abraham's encounter with God he says to Sarah, his wife, "Honey, I just had a little talk with God, and God wants us to pick up our possessions and move to a foreign land where we don't know a living soul. But don't worry, the good news is that I will be blessed and God through me will make a great nation." Sarah replies, "Sweetheart, that sounds like a terrific idea. It is logical and makes sense. I will start packing so we can get an early start in the morning." That is not exactly what happened. It was much more likely that Abraham responded, "Lord, you want me to do what and go where?" And Sarah replied, "You are not dragging me halfway around the world. If you are going you are going by yourself."

Later, in regard to the birth of their son, their response was one of laughter. Abraham actually fell down on his face and laughed when he heard these words and he said to God, "Will a son be born to a man who is 100 years old? Will Sarah bear a child at the age of 90?" Frederick Buechner visions Sarah as sitting in her rocking chair crocheting as she overhears the conversation between her husband and God and she nearly falls out of the chair with laughter. No wonder she laughed, because she was about to have one foot in the maternity ward and the other in the grave. It was a cynical laugh. They laughed because God expected them to believe it. They laughed because God seemed to believe it. They laughed because they half believed it themselves. They laughed to keep from crying. After hearing their laughter God said to Abraham, "Is anything too hard for the Lord?"

God's promise was a struggle for them because they found the promise to be beyond reason and belief. The promise that God had given to them conflicted with reality. The fact is, how could Abraham be the father of a great nation when he had no son? His wife Sarah was well beyond childbearing age. Humanly speaking there was no hope of this promise coming true. It seemed foolish and absurd. Brueggemann points out that this story is constructed to present the tension between the inscrutable speech of God and the resistance and mockery of Abraham and Sarah, who doubt the word and cannot believe the promise. "Once again the story shows what a scandal and difficulty faith is ... Abraham and Sarah by this time have become accustomed to their barrenness. They are resigned to their closed future. They have accepted that hopelessness as 'normal' ... It is rejected as nonsensical" (Brueggemann, *Genesis*, p. 158f). At this point Abraham was not fully convinced that God was able to do what God had promised as stated in Romans 4:21.

Adjusting To Things As They Are

Abraham's social security checks came each month through direct deposit. They enjoyed their AARP discounts. In the cold winters they traveled south to the warm waters of the sunny Mediterranean coasts. In the hot summers they traveled to the cool breezes of the Judean mountain area. Abraham and Sarah liked the predictability of their lives, so they laughed at God's promise and offer. They resigned themselves to their closed, barren future. In effect they said, "Lord, we have never done it this way before and we are not about to start now." They were willing to accept their hopelessness as normal. They adjusted to things as they were.

Abraham did not want anything new. They wanted to fall back on the old. Why? It is obvious: the old is predictable, familiar, and reassuring. The new and the future are an unknown quantity, strange and threatening. God says to Abraham, "I am taking a new direction and you are part of it. You will be the father of a great nation and Sarah will bear a son and pave the way for the new to come." Not only did Abraham laugh, but he says, "I have Ishmael; he will do." Abraham is no longer pressed to believe in an heir that is to be given, for he already has one. At this point he is willing to stake his future on Ishmael. Abraham sticks with the old, the known and the predictable, rather than trust the new and unknown.

But God said to Abraham, "No, Ishmael will not do. Sarah will bear you a son and he will be the child of covenant." Do you see what is happening here? What God is offering to Abraham is a shift in the root of his identity. Instead of identifying himself through the clan, family, and the culture in Haran, he is now to identfiy himself through the new covenant with God.

A Leap Of Faith

The question was put to Abraham, "Is anything too hard for the Lord?" To Abraham there were many things that seemed impossible regarding God's promise to him. So many obstacles seemed to stand in the way for the promise of the covenant to ever take place. From his human point of view there was no way possible that this promise could ever be fulfilled. Then God asked that poignant question, "Is anything to hard for the Lord?" If so, then not even God can change one's situation. If there are things in one's life that are impossible for God to do, then life is a closed universe, where God is not present with little possibility for change. Then life is characterized by "whatever will be will be," where one becomes the victim of whatever happens to come along. If, on the other hand, "nothing is impossible for God," then life is full of endless possibilities. There is no door that cannot be opened, no obstacle that cannot be overcome, nothing in life that is beyond God's power.

After a great struggle, even to the point of laughing at God, now Abraham through faith is going to make a venture into the unknown. His decision may appear to many as unreasonable, bordering on foolishness. Faith for Abraham now, after a long struggle of coping with doubt, results in his willingness to trust God even in the face of evidence that is baffling, ambiguous, and contradictory. But now he is about to make a leap of faith and take God at his word. He believes God's promise to him, and Sarah conceives, and Isaac is born. I can visualize how she walks into the Tuesday morning bridge club meeting with her bassinet holding little Isaac. Everyone had a great time laughing with Sarah — laughing at God's ability to work wonders. This was not the cynical laughter of Sarah earlier, but this is the laughter that comes from the unexpected intrusions of a living and loving God. God's promises are true, and the joke is on us and we laugh.

Abraham had no idea how long a shadow he was going to cast — what a profound effect his life would have on others. This nomadic Semite left Haran in upper Mesopotomia and went to Palestine. On the face of it, an unremarkable event, yet for Jew and Christian a movement fraught with destiny for the whole human race. Paul's emphasis in the text is that it was not the keeping of the law but Abraham's faith and God's grace and it "was reckoned to him as righteousness." It was God's grace and Abraham's faith that made it all possible. In the text Paul by using his example of Abraham is setting before the Romans two illustrations. In one, we see Abraham who is seeking to have a right relationship with God through his own efforts which was doomed to failure. Then through Abraham's faith a new relationship with God becomes possible.

Much of Abraham's struggle is the essence of our struggles as well. When God comes calling we do not drop everything and follow. For most there is resistance and rebellion. There are many who have not yet responded, others who are still rebelling and resisting. We may be more like Jonah than Abraham, people on the run. In hearing God's promise you respond much like Abraham, feeling that God's promise for your life conflicts with reality and outdistances your ability to believe it or understand it. But when Abraham resisted, God's question to him was: "Is anything too hard for the Lord?" That is the question we need to ask.

25

Lent 3

The Scandal
Of The Cross

1 Corinthians 1:18-25

The preaching of the cross in the first century world was repulsive and odious. The insistence that a man tried, convicted, and executed for a capital crime is the savior of the world is scandalous. Paul describes it in our text as being "a stumbling block to Jews and foolishness to Gentiles" (v. 23).

The Cross As Foolishness

First, Paul declares that the cross to the Greek mind appeared as foolishness. Why? Because to the Greek mind, deity is seen as one of power, being free from pain, suffering, and death. They developed elaborate philosophical arguments to prove that their god must be free from distress and that such a deity was never moved by compassion to assist human brokenness and despair. To show compassion toward the poor or powerless was a sign of weakness. The Greek god could not suffer as men and women do. Therefore, to the Greek mind it was unthinkable that a son of God, having divine characteristics, could endure death like a criminal. A crucified God was repulsive to the Greeks.

Ernest Campbell tells about a young doctor who had no time for God or the church. It so happened that he visited a leprosarium in Africa and asked the sister who was in charge how many patients she had in the institution. "Sixty," she replied. "Your God must feel pain and disappointment when he looks at this world of sickness," the doctor answered. "But," the sister said, "God does not feel pain or disappointment when he looks at this world of

27

pain." Whereupon the doctor declared, "Perhaps that is why I don't care to believe in him."

The truth is that God does feel pain. Look at today's Old Testament lesson from Exodus 3. "Then the Lord said, 'I have observed the misery of my people who are in Egypt; I have heard their cry on account of their taskmasters. Indeed, I know their suffering ...' " (Exodus 3:7). In Christ, God comes to where people hope and suffer. The central theme of the New Testament is that "the word became flesh and dwelt among us, full of grace and truth ... " (John 1:14). Jesus knew life as we know life. Therefore, we can cry from the depths of our despair, "O Lord, you know how it is!" He does, because he dwelt among us. This is what the incarnation is all about.

Still, crucifixion was repugnant to the first century world. There were three means of capital punishment in first century Palestine: stoning, beheading, and crucifixion. All are mentioned in the New Testament: Stephen was stoned, John the Baptist was beheaded, and Jesus was crucified. Crucifixion was administered to the most dangerous criminals. It was used mainly for guerrilla insurrectionists who took up arms against the Romans. Jesus, who never took up arms or advocated that others do so, was regarded as sufficiently dangerous to merit this extreme form of execution. Therein is the scandal of the cross.

The Cross As A Stumbling Block
The cross to the Jewish mind was a stumbling block. Why? They looked for a Messiah who would be known by signs in heaven and on earth. The Messiah would destroy all other gods and drive all the foreigners from the land with a power similar to or mightier than David and Solomon, a Lord "mighty in battle."

The Jewish mind questioned how this lowly Jesus of Nazareth, who was born in obscurity to humble parents and who associated with the poor and outcast, could be the Messiah. He did not destroy the foreign armies. He did not demonstrate political power, but rather servitude and self-giving, which was interpreted as weakness. He did not overcome the enemies of Israel, but he was scorned, maltreated, and put to death as a most dangerous lawbreaker.

28

For both the Greek and the Jew death is the ultimate weakness. How could this be of God? There the cross is both foolishness and a stumbling block.

The Cross In Today's World

The most important question does not concern the cross in the ancient world, but the cross in our world. A recent comment on this passage by Nathan Williams made me aware of the ease with which we display the cross in our world. What in the first century was a hideous instrument of execution today hangs from our necks on chains, adorns the lapels of our jackets, dangles from our wrists on bracelets, and is seen as frosting on Lenten hot cross buns (*Expository Times,* March 1983, p. 329). We have domesticated the cross. We have tried to make it less offensive and scandalous. The cross is so offensive that some have sought to avoid it in their theology. A crossless Christianity has had great appeal and it has gained a substantial following and popularity. Yet the cross stands in the center of our chancels. It is, indeed, the central symbol of Christianity. Yet the cross is difficult for us to understand — difficult to talk about and difficult to preach about.

However, it is part of the biblical record. A man who was tried, convicted, and executed for a capital crime is the Savior of the world. It is remarkable how we make such a public display of the cross, but at the same time the cross of Christ has such little influence on our public lives. Thomas à Kempis, who lived and wrote in the Middle Ages, speaks of us when he said, "Jesus has many who love his kingdom, but few who bear his cross. Many are willing to rejoice with him, but few are willing to suffer with him."

Many have asked: Why did God do it this way? Look at verse 29 in the text, "So that no one might boast in the presence of God." Salvation for our world is not by intellect or wisdom or from the profound thinkers of the day. If so, masses of ordinary people would never have known God's love and power in their lives. The apostle declares: "God chose what is foolish in the world to shame the wise; God chose what is weak in the world to shame the strong; God chose what is low and despised in the world, things that are not, to reduce to nothing the things that are" (vv. 27-28). Obviously, God's purpose was to base the faith of men and women not on human cleverness, but on the saving power through Christ. That's why Paul concludes this section, "Let him who boasts, boast in the Lord."

What counts in life is not the pride of intellect, civic position, or prestige, but the saving grace of God revealed through a crucified God. The ancient hymn captures the essence of this truth: "In the cross of Christ I glory. Towering o'er the wrecks of time." Frederick Buechner points out that the symbols of other religions, such as the six-pointed star, the crescent moon, and the lotus flower, are symbols that suggest light and beauty. "The symbol of Christianity is the instrument of death. It suggests, at the very least, hope" (Buechner, *Wishful Thinking*, p. 19).

The respected sociologist Robert Bellah and his colleagues wrote a very revealing book, *The Habits of the Heart,* showing how our individualism has led to isolation and fragmentation in our society and that our generation has become self-centered, narcissistic, and excessively materialistic. The cross and the crucifixion are offensive to such lifestyles. To the modern mind anything that smacks of weakness, poverty, or servitude is regarded as being repulsive.

The apostle clearly understands how the cross appears to many as folly, foolishness, and weakness. He is convinced that it is the secret to understanding the wisdom of God, "for God's foolishness is wiser than human wisdom." Only the God of the New Testament is foolish enough to become one with those who suffer and die. To believe that God really was "in Christ" is to believe that God is intentionally with all who suffer. The cross tells us that in our loss, tragedy, or pains our God is there before us. There are footprints in the sand. Conventional wisdom has no room for such nonsense.

Where Is God?

Elie Wiesel, a survivor of Auschwitz, gives this vivid account in his book *Night.* The electric power station at Buna was blown up and the Gestapo followed a trail that led to two men and a boy back at the Auschwitz camp. The SS sentenced them to death and ordered all the prisoners out on the parade grounds to witness the hangings. There was total silence among the prisoners as they were about to be hanged. No one moved or said a word as the prisoners were led to the gallows. When the trap door opened beneath their feet the two men died almost instantly. But the boy, because he lacked the body weight of the men, struggled for his life for nearly half an hour. The SS made all of the prisoners stay and watch the boy's struggle. Wiesel said that someone in the back of the crowd cried out, "Where is God? Where is God now?" Wiesel said, "I heard a voice within me answer him, 'Where is God? He is hanging there on the gallows.' " He went on to say that "at that moment to speak of a God who could not suffer would make God a demon."

Where is God in all that is transpiring in our lives and in our world? Today it may not be Auschwitz, but Bosnia, Rwanda, and Kosovo, or the blood-spattered campuses of our schools from Oregon to Arkansas as teenage violence continues to ravage our land bringing havoc and pain to so many, or a landscape that has been ravaged by a tornado or hurricane which leaves destruction and death in its wake. The cross tells us where God is. God has entered into our suffering and has experienced it all before us. God, through Jesus, knew suffering, sadness, rejection, and pain as we do, and God experienced death, which comes to all of us. So the God we turn to in our distress is the God with a human face. The God who bids us to come to him has his arms outstretched and his hands bear the marks of the nail prints. He opens his heart of love and grace to us, a heart scarred by the piercing of a sword. No matter what darkness or sadness enters our lives, the cross casts its shadow, which reminds us that God has been there before us.

Where is God? Right where God has always been — loving and caring for his own!

Amazing Grace

Ephesians 2:1-10

Keith Miller, a well-known author and Episcopal church-
man, arrived in Bloomington, Illinois, for a speaking engagement.
He got to town the night before he was to speak so he bought a
local newspaper to catch up on the local news. Close to Bloomington
were two towns: Oblong and Normal. To his surprise the head-
lines on the society page read: "Oblong Man Marries Normal
Woman." He thought that was hilarious. In the pulpit the next
morning he told the congregation what he had read in the society
section of the newspaper the night before. No one laughed. No
one even made a snicker. They had grown so accustomed and
familiar to those phrases and words that they didn't appear as hu-
morous to the local people.

Grace Is A Key Word
    It is easy to allow words and phrases to lose their meaning.
We become so accustomed to them they no longer seem significant. This is always possible for words and phrases we use over
and over again. This is the danger we face in our constant use of
both the Apostles' Creed and the Lord's Prayer, the possibility of
reducing them to mere words and phrases. Our faith would be
impoverished if we lost the meaning of some key words. The
word *grace* is one of the key words in our biblical and theological
vocabulary. It is an important word because it helps us to understand our relationship with God and with one another. Notice
how critical and significant it is in our text: "For by *grace* you
have been saved through faith ..." Philip Yancey said that he keeps

circling back to the word *grace* because it is one grand theological word that has not been spoiled. He calls it the "the last best word" because every English usage that he finds contains something of the original meaning. "Like a vast aquifer, the word underlies our proud civilization, reminding us that good things come not from our own efforts, rather by the grace of God" (Philip Yancey, *What Is So Amazing About Grace?* p. 12).

Grace is not a salvation by works. But a salvation by works and deeds is simple and clear and easy to grasp. This is how we deal with one another. Individuals earn our respect and love. It is not something that we freely give. We do not respond positively to people we do not know. As we are accustomed to having people prove themselves to us before we are willing to accept them, some feel this is also true in our relationship with God. As we prove ourselves to God, then God will like us and care for us. Because of our ignorance regarding grace, there is that prevailing attitude among us that we must earn God's favor. Thus, a salvation by works and deeds is easier for us to grasp and understand, since this is basically how we deal with one another in our human relationships.

Sometime ago I talked with a church member who left no doubt in my mind that he considered himself better than many and superior to most. As a socially prominent person he saw his success and fortune as the favor of God. As our conversation continued I was disheartened by his derogatory comments regarding the poor and less fortunate people in the community. He didn't have the slightest understanding of the meaning of grace. I was reminded of Archibald MacLeish's comments before the graduating class at McGill University: "Never think too much of money and position, for someday you will meet a person for whom this means nothing. Then you will realize how poor you really are." In Christ, we have met such a person.

A Grace-Filled Life

A person who thinks that he or she has earned a good grade before God, even a passing grade, has never encountered the God of the Bible. They have not yet seen the Lord high and lifted up.

They have not yet recognized themselves for what they are — sinners in need of the grace of God. If you are the recipient of grace then the magnitude of this experience is too overwhelming; it causes you to realize that you have received what you did not merit and could never have possibly earned. When such *amazing grace* is experienced and affirmed, then humility and generosity are the results. Smugness, arrogance, and superiority are not the characteristics of a grace-filled life. How is it that Saint Francis of Assisi, Mother Teresa, Nelson Mandela, or Bishop Tutu could have such little regard for themselves and give so much of themselves to other people and their needs? They seem to say with the hymn writer, "What a debt to grace I owe."

There is a deep-rooted conviction that is held by many that one has to earn and work for one's passage into the kingdom of God. The case is made by declaring: "Lord, I am a decent sort of person. I have done my best to fulfill my religious duties. At least I am better than most. I don't get roaring drunk, beat my wife, or abuse my children. My pledge to the church isn't much, but at least I pay it. I mind my own business, and I don't get involved in other people's lives or in the needs of others because religion is a private affair. Lord, I think that this should provide some special attention on my account." I am certain that God has heard that prayer often. The apostle's reply in our text is, "You've got it all wrong — for by grace are you saved through faith, and this is not your own doing; it is the gift of God."

Grace is not based on merit, need, or appeal. This is true, however, of our relationships with one another. "I'll do for you if you do for me." "I'll scratch your back if you scratch mine." Many of our relations are based on *merit*. Michael Jordan is one of the highest-paid professional athletes in the world. He has demanded millions from the Chicago Bulls basketball team. The Bulls through the years have met his financial demands. Do the Bulls pay him well because they have a particular fondness for him? No. They pay him millions because he can put the ball in the hoop and win championships for the Bulls. This relationship between Michael Jordan and the Chicago Bulls is based on merit.

35

Many of our relationships are based on *need.* I keep on good terms with my automobile mechanic, especially since I drive an older truck with well over 100,000 miles on it. It has been said that there are two ways to lose your life's savings: go to the race track or take your car into the garage for repairs. If you have a good mechanic who is honest, dependable, and reasonable you have a rare find. I need my mechanic because he can fix my carburetor and do it right the first time. Our relationship is based on need.

Other relationships are based on *appeal.* A man does not love a woman because she can fix carburetors or slam dunk basketballs, but because he finds her charming, attractive, and appealing. This is the kind of person with whom he wants to spend the rest of his life. Take away the merit, need, and appeal and these relationships would dissolve. The relationship between God and ourselves is unlike these relationships, because it is based on *grace.* God does not enter into personal relationships with us because God needs us — God doesn't — nor because we are good — we are not. Our relationship with God is not based on the fact that we offer anything to God, but on the fact that God offers everything to us.

Grace Through Faith

Therefore, grace is the unmerited, unearned, undeserved goodness of God offered to us in Jesus Christ. *For by grace — you have been saved — through faith* — these nine mono-syllables have a special cadence, movement, and rhythm resonating over and over again from the first century until the present. Do you sense the lyrical movement of these words and what they meant to the apostle Paul who penned them? Every time the Church discovers these words, they produce revival, reformation, and transformation. The idea of grace disappeared from the Church until Augustine brought it back in the fifth century, and it was rediscovered by Luther in the sixteenth century and again by Wesley in the eighteenth century. Every time the Church got off track, the words of the text, the rediscovery of God's grace in Jesus Christ got the Church back on track. H. Richard Niebuhr reminds us that "the great Christian revolutions come not by the discovery of something that was not known before. They happen when somebody takes radically something that was always there." Today we need to rediscover *grace* as the unmerited, unearned, undeserved love of God offered to us in Jesus Christ and once again allow grace to do its radical work among us in both our hearts and society.

Never has there been a time, on such a wide scale, that men and women have been more baffled, dismayed, despondent, and discouraged by the demise of the human person. Never has the world experienced on such a wide scale the sheer irrationality of the evil things humans can do to each other. We are about to close the most violent century in our history. Many of us have lived through these darkest moments in human experience — the Holocaust and World War II. We now know what Luther meant when he said in his great hymn, "Though this world with devils filled should threaten to undo us." We have seen the "dark side" of life. We confront it every day in the newspaper and on television. The apostle reminds us that "by grace" we can recover our destiny. Even in a demonic world men and women may choose to "live by grace through faith." Luther did say, "Though this world with devils filled should threaten to undo us," but he went on to say, "We will not fear, for God hath willed his truth to triumph through us."

Grace is what God brings to us at the point of our deepest need. God does not deal with us according to what we deserve, but according to what we need. That's grace! Grace is the way God offers himself to us. Through grace God comes to us on the level of our need, where we are, and looks into our eyes. God does not ask us to clean ourselves up or straighten ourselves out before coming. That is the very thing we cannot do and that is why we so desperately need grace. God asks us, "Where does it hurt and how can I help?" He comes to us at the level of our need. That is what's so amazing about grace!

Grace Through Christ

Barclay, in his autobiography, said that the most important passage in the entire Bible for him is John 1:14, "The word became flesh and lived among us ... full of grace and truth." He went on to say that the evidence of God's grace was seen in Christ who took the entire weight of human sorrow, anguish, and sin upon himself as expressed in the concise statement of our ancient creed: "crucified, dead, and buried." Luther, in the second verse of his mighty hymn, reminds us:

> *Were not the right man on our side,*
> *The man of God's own choosing,*
> *Dost ask who that may be?*
> *Christ Jesus, it is he ...*
> *And he must win the battle.*

The gap between ourselves and God has been spanned, not by pushing out the frail bridge of our own good works, but by God who crosses the gap to meet us in Jesus Christ.

Why wasn't Jacob cast by God on the scrap heap for his warped and twisted ways? Why wasn't David disowned by God for his immoral and degrading deeds against Uriah and his wife? Why wasn't Peter left to sink because of his base denial of Christ? Why wasn't Saul of Tarsus, persecutor, blasphemer, and hater of Christ, blotted out from the book of life forever? Why does God allow this dismal, despairing world to blow itself to pieces to the delight of some of our neo-apocalyptic preachers of doom? Why is it that God has not given up on you and me who reject his love and pollute his earth? Why? I'll tell you why. Because there is nothing on earth so dogged, determined, stubborn, and persistent as the grace of God who seeks to save. This grace is unmerited, unearned, undeserved. At times it is surprising, even astonishing, but it is always an amazing grace!

The Right Person For The Job

Hebrews 5:5-10

Consideration is being given today to the *teaching sermon*. By the nature of certain texts a specific sermon can have both teaching and learning as its fundamental purpose. (See Ronald J. Allen's *The Teaching Sermon*, Abingdon Press, 1995.) The reason that this text lends itself to teaching and learning is the result of two ideas that we are introduced to by the writer of Hebrews, namely the high priest and the person called Melchizedek. The broadening of our understanding of these two subjects will enrich and deepen our understanding of Jesus' life, teaching, and death during our Lenten pilgrimage.

Jesus As High Priest

The writer of Hebrews wants us to know that Jesus is now the great high priest. He claims that Jesus is the kind of great high priest who carries our deepest sorrows and most earnest prayers to the very throne of God. He points out that Jesus is the only great high priest because he is without sin (14:15) and Jesus does for us what we cannot attain for ourselves. Although Jesus was without sin, the writer points out that it in no way took away from his humanity, but rather it affirms that Jesus experienced the full ambiguity and uncertainty, the weakness and the vulnerability, the temptations and the suffering of life without compromising his humanity. Thomas Long points out that those who listen to the writer of Hebrews are well aware that Jesus died on the cross, and the question for them was whether this weak and suffering Jesus is also the divine Son of God. "They are well aware that Jesus was a fellow sufferer in ways the eye cannot see, and stands in graceful glory at the beginning and end of time, and even in the middle of time and is even now redeeming the creation and bringing the children of God home" (Thomas J. Long, *Hebrews*, p. 65).

The writer of Hebrews (I say writer because only God knows who wrote Hebrews) is well aware that the people knew about Jesus' suffering and death on the cross. The question for them is: "If he is the high priest, what kind of high priest must he be?" Long suggests that the author approaches this dilemma by giving them the "right person for the job" speech. He presents the provisions for the job description and shows how Jesus meets the qualifications perfectly and that Jesus is indeed the great high priest. Jesus not only fulfills the qualifications but he exceeds them. The point for the writer is: "Jesus is not just the high priest, he is, in fact, 'the great high priest' " (Long, *Hebrews*, p. 66). Notice how the writer lists the three basic qualifications for the ancient high priest, then in reverse order reveals how Jesus exceeds each one of them.

The high priest:
1. Function of the high priest (v. 1).
2. Person of the high priest (vv. 2-3).
3. Appointment of the high priest (v. 4).

Jesus as high priest:
1. Appointment of Jesus as high priest (vv. 5-6).
2. Person of Jesus as great high priest (vv. 7-8).
3. Functions of Jesus as great high priest (vv. 9-10).

Therefore, as we approach our text as one that lends itself to a teaching and instructional sermon, let us consider the following.

The Function Of The High Priest

The function of the high priest was to serve as the go-between, the mediator between God and the people. He is appointed on behalf of the people to deal with the things concerning God. For Israel the high priest had one primary function: to offer sacrifice for the sins of the people (5:1). The sacrifice made by the high priest is meant to restore the relationship between God and the people, which had been broken by human sin. The high priest is the messenger of salvation, carrying on behalf of the people symbols of repentance to God and returning to the people with the assurance of divine forgiveness. Scholars point out that Jesus exceeds the ancient high priests in at least two ways. First, he is not just mediator, but he is the source of salvation (5:9). Second, the old high priest had to keep coming back time and again to the altar — new sins, new sacrifices — but the salvation provided through the high priestly ministry of Jesus is eternal (5:9). The New Testament message is that Christ offered himself "once and for all" for the sins of all people (1 Peter 3:18).

The function of the high priest is to stand before God with his back to the people. Then he comes before the people with his back towards God, facing the people on behalf of God. "The priest represents God's holy presence among the people" (Long, *Hebrews*, 65). When Jesus the great high priest stands before the people, what do the people see? In the face of Jesus "is the reflection of God's glory and the exact imprint of God's very being ..." (Hebrews 1:3a). Jesus puts a face on God, "for in him the whole fullness of the deity dwells bodily" (Colossians 2:9). Paul states this so eloquently: "He is the image of the invisible God" (Colossians 1:15). When Jesus stands before the people as the great high priest, the people see in his face a God who stoops down from the holy heights to bear our griefs and carry our sorrows. "But he was wounded for our transgressions, crushed for our iniquities, upon him was the punishment that made us whole, and by his bruises we are made whole" (Isaiah 53:5). In the face of Jesus, the high priest, the people see a God to whom they can pray freely and confidently so that we can "receive mercy and find grace in the time of need" (Hebrews 4:16).

The Person Of The High Priest
The person who functions as the high priest in ancient Israel was a person who needed to possess certain qualities of personality and compassion. They were people who needed to know about the pain and struggles of human life and to be sympathetic to human weaknesses. When they were making a sacrifice for someone, it

meant that they were aware of the deepest secrets of life. They were confronted with confused and sinful people and they needed a sympathetic and loving heart so as to minister to them with gentleness and understanding. A high priest was a very special person in the Jewish religious community. The high priests were every bit as sinful as their flocks, and as they approached the altar, they did so carrying the sacrifices for their own sins as well as for the sins of others (5:2-3).

It is necessary for the high priest to know the experiences that the people have gone through. He needs to be aware of the deep secrets of life: the sin, guilt, fear, disappointment, hope, and hunger for salvation that was so much a part of the masses. The priest must be one with the people. Barclay points out that "the priest must be bound up with men in the bundle of life" (Barclay, *Hebrews,* p. 46). The priest needs to possess the ability to bear with people without getting irritated; it means the ability not to lose one's temper with people when they are foolish and will not learn and do the same things over and over again (5:2). Through sympathy and understanding the high priest is a person who constantly and patiently seeks to lead the people back to the right way.

The author of Hebrews, after giving the qualifications of the high priest, states: "So also Christ did not glorify himself in becoming a high priest, but was appointed by the one who said to him, 'You are my Son, today I have begotten you' " (v. 5). The author now points out how Jesus fulfills the great conditions for the priesthood. He came from among the people and knew and experienced every aspect of human life. If the high priest is one who should know his people, then Jesus through the incarnation is the epitome of what a high priest should be. Through Jesus God comes to us where we are.

Jesus labored as a tradesman in his father's carpenter shop, he knew firsthand about irritable customers and at times found it hard to collect his bills and make ends meet. He shared the anguish of parents over the death of their child; he suffered in the despair of the unemployed in the marketplace. He knew the plight of the poor and the shame of the outcast. He identified with the "undesirables." He grieved over the stubbornness of men and women. He laughed with little children. He died bleeding, but not before he had felt our ultimate doubt when he cried, "My God, my God, why have you forsaken me?" He was "crucified, dead, and buried" — a phrase which is the blunt statement of the creed regarding his humanness. That Jesus came to share our lives there is no doubt. The Jewish requirement of a high priest is that he must be a person who knows and represents the people — Jesus far exceeds the qualifications. There is no doubt that he is *the right person for the job.*

The Appointment Of The High Priest
No one in ancient Israel would be so presumptuous as to volunteer for the position of high priest. No one would ever appoint himself to the priesthood. It is not a position that a man takes; it is a privilege and a glory to which he is called. Barclay points out that "a ministry of God among people is neither a job nor a career, but a calling" (Barclay, *Hebrews*, p. 47). This is even true for Jesus; he did not choose his task. God chose him for it. At his baptism there came the voice to Jesus saying, "You are my Son, the Beloved; with you I am well pleased" (Mark 1:11).

The author of Hebrews is convinced that Jesus is well prepared to be the great high priest, because he has gone through the most bitter experiences of men and women and he understands, as no other, the human family's strengths and weaknesses. It appears that in verses 8-9, the author is reflecting upon Jesus' experience in Gethsemane. Scholars point out that the words that are used in verse 7, "loud cries," come from the Greek that refers to a cry which a man does not choose to utter but which is wrung from him in the stress of some tremendous tension or searing pain. The author indicates in verse 8 that Jesus "learned obedience through what he suffered," pointing out that Jesus learned from all of his experiences because he met them all with reverence. By these experiences of pain and suffering "having been made perfect, he became the source of eternal salvation for all who obey him." (vv. 8-9). The writer of Hebrews is saying that all the experiences of suffering that Jesus experienced prepared him to become the great high priest, the Savior of men and women. Jesus is not a high priest for a lifetime, but forever, and not according to the regular orders of the priesthood, but "having been designated by God a high priest according to the order of Melchizedek." Again, Jesus exceeds the job description of the high priest and is no doubt — *the right man for the job.*

To both the author's congregation and our congregations the people are not certain about what the references to Melchizedek are all about. Both his congregation and our congregations need an explanation. The point that the author of Hebrews makes regarding Melchizedek is clear. He states that way back in the days of Abraham before the Levitical priesthood, there appeared a foreshadowing of Jesus becoming the great high priest. This foreshadowing was Melchizedek. He was the King of Salem, meaning "king of righteousness" and "king of peace." This anticipates Jesus' messanic role as the king of righteousness and peace (7:2).

According to the author of Hebrews, Melchizedek further anticipated Jesus by the fact that he had no mother or father, thus no genealogy. He was totally without beginning and end in time (7:3). "The main point in all of this is not really about Melchizedek, but rather how the qualities seen in him — righteousness, peace and timeless — point forward to the nature of Jesus, the true and perpetual great high priest. The author sees Melchizedek as a signpost planted in the old order indicating that the good gifts given to humanity in Jesus were there in God's mind from the beginning" (Long, *Hebrews,* p. 85).

Through the incarnation Jesus knows the pain and ambiguity of human life. The difference between the high priests and Jesus the great high priest is that Jesus reveals a God who cares desperately, a God who, through Jesus, is involved in every aspect of human life. Barbara Taylor Brown reminds us that "when you look at him (Jesus) you see God. When you listen to him, you hear God. Not because he has taken God's place, but because he is the clear window that God has glazed into flesh and blood — the porthole between this world and the next, the passageway between heaven and earth" (*The Preaching Life*, p. 23). By Jesus, the high priest, offering himself as "ransom for many" the human family is healed, and men and women, though ravaged and broken, now can become what God intended at creation, free and joyful — at one with oneself, with one another, with creation, and with God.

Symbols Of
Hope And Reality

Philippians 2:5-11

We are about to embark on Holy Week. A period of time
that will allow us to walk where Jesus walked. A time when we
will go from the Upper Room through the Via Dolorosa to Golgotha
and to the gravesite on Easter morning. We hope, during this journey, to gain insight to the heart and mind of Christ. How fortunate
if we could gain some insight to Jesus' compassion, love, and grace,
and to his self-giving creating in us something of the mind of Christ.

The form that Paul uses in our text is a hymn. It is not certain
whether Paul composed it or if it is one already known by the
Philippian Church. Craddock points out that the majority opinion
is that Paul is quoting a hymn which arose in another context to
address another problem, perhaps a christological question. It was
not uncommon to quote from such a hymn from a common source
of material used for worship in the Gentile churches. "It is a hymn
that expresses the Christ story in movements: pre-existence, existence, and post-existence" (Fred Craddock, *Philippians,* John Knox
Press, p. 40). By quoting this hymn, the church is reminded of the
event that created and defined their life together. The apostle is
saying to the congregation that in their life together they need to
think this way, "Let the same mind be in you that was in Christ
Jesus" (v. 5).

Many scholars feel that this is the most moving passage that
Paul ever wrote about Jesus. His desire was for this congregation
to capture the essence of the life of Christ. He wanted them to
shed their personal ambitions of power and position, and humble
themselves, gaining a selfless desire to serve as he set forth for

them the example of Christ. He wrote this passage so that they would lay aside all discord, personal ambitions, and pride, and live in harmony by becoming Christlike. He points out that Christ had taken the initiative: "And being found in human form, he humbled himself and became obedient to the point of death — even death on a cross" (v. 8).

The Ordinariness Of God

As we make this journey during Holy Week, one thing that will stand out in the life of Jesus is that he was "being found in human form" (v. 7b). There was an ordinariness about that life of Christ that we find difficult. In Christ, God becomes so near and ordinary "being found in human form." This is exactly why the hometown folks in Mark 6 had such difficulty in accepting Jesus as Messiah. He was too much like them. If this was God, then God was too down-to-earth. The town folks spoke up, saying, "We know who he is. He is not fooling us. He is the carpenter's son. That is Joseph's boy." This meant that he was from the side streets of Nazareth. He was from the industrial park area where he lived over the carpenter shop with his family. Immediately, this brings to mind train tracks, warehouses, cement mixers, asphalt plants, signs, and billboards. The folks of Nazareth said among themselves, "He is from the lower order. What does he know?"

You see, they had the facts on him. They knew his origins, his family, his name, and his occupation. There are those who, knowing the origin of someone, are convinced they understand all there is to know about that person. They are convinced that people from certain locations, families, races, cultures, or backgrounds are all alike and that no one of any importance can come from those kinds of roots. We have heard it all before, haven't we? As far as Jesus is concerned, they had the facts on him, but they did not really know him.

That day in Nazareth they stumbled over the truth because it appeared so ordinary, so obvious and familiar. Fred Craddock tells how, upon the death of a saint, those who visited his home after his death were surprised to find a broom, detergents, trash cans, old newspapers, an ironing board, dirty dishes, a worn sweater, toilet tissue, a can of tuna, Sweet and Low, and utility bills. With astonishment they gasped, "He was just like us!" How hard it is for us to realize that liberation comes to us on limping, human feet! It is hard for us to realize that God's presence among us is to be "found in human form."

The Need For A Sign

Holy Week is a time for us to enter into the life of Christ more deeply. Not only to remember his "being found in human form," but to capture the essence of the life of Christ and to see how he shed any desires for personal power and position, humbling himself to become the selfless servant of others. We must remember how essential it is for us to have this "same mind in you (us) that was in Christ Jesus" (v. 5), so that we, like the Philippians, will lay aside our discord and pride and live in harmony by becoming Christlike. From the experiences of Holy Week, especially Maundy Thursday and Good Friday, we are left with vivid and rich symbols of hope and reality that will greatly help us in our desire to allow the mind of Christ to be in us.

Jesus etched some things indelibly upon our minds. He knew that he would be arrested and betrayed and that his friends would be scattered. After all that had happened how could he help them to remember his life and his death and what it all meant? How could they remember who they were called to be? A sign was needed that they could incorporate into their daily schedule. That evening in the Upper Room he took bread because it was so common. It was shared and eaten every day. He broke it, and while he shared it with his disciples he said, "Remember me when you share bread." He wanted them to remember every day at mealtime when they took the bread and broke it, to be reminded of his body which was broken for them. Then he took the cup of wine saying, "This cup which is poured out for you is the new covenant in my blood."

Bread And Wine

Think of the lowliness and humbleness that are reflected in these two symbols. Their appropriateness are seen in the words of the prophet, "he had no form or majesty" (Isaiah 53:2b). The symbols that Jesus presented to his disciples in the Upper Room were not monuments in stone, no massive shrine, but merely bread and wine. Consider how commonplace they are — they link Jesus with every home. Consider their appropriateness. The bread comes from the seed that died to live, and the wine was wrung from the winepress. People will quarrel over creeds and doctrines, but who could quarrel over bread and wine? By taking the bread and wine we have an opportunity to transcend our differences and discover our unity in Jesus Christ as our Lord. I was pastor of a United Methodist church in Miami that was a multiracial and multicultural congregation. Not everyone spoke English. Because of our history of depending on verbal communication, basically English, many people could not understand or participate in the service. Many felt awkward and strange. When we decided to celebrate the sacrament at every service, we immediately communicated, and all were able to participate. When each person took in his or her hands the bread and the cup, it communicated in a very dramatic and vivid way the presence of Jesus Christ among us. Our cultural and racial differences sought to divide us, but our sharing together in the body of Christ united us. The sacrament of the bread and cup provided for us a non-verbal means of communication that was powerful.

The Towel And Basin

Jesus gave us the sign of the towel and basin. Just after the feast of the Passover, when Jesus knew that the end was near and knowing that he had come from God and was going to go to God, he got up from supper and laid aside his garments. He then girded himself with a towel and took a basin and filled it with water. He proceeded to wash the disciples' feet and wipe them with a towel. Notice the sequence of events here. It was just after the disciples had a quarrel as to which of them was the greatest. Think how Jesus must have felt. He was facing Jerusalem, and the cross was imminent, and his disciples were arguing about who was the greatest. Dramatically, he takes a basin full of water and washes the disciples' feet. Jesus declared that the greatest of all is the servant of all, and he said, "I am in the midst of you as one who serves."

It appears that in the chronology of the synoptic gospels this event took place immediately following the Lord's Supper. They were still under the spell of Jesus' words and actions at the table as they were sharing the cup and loaf together. But the mood was rudely broken. Jesus moved swiftly from the table to the towel and the basin. It tells us the kind of Lord we worship and serve. Jesus dramatically brought together faith and ethics, belief and behavior, piety and service, prayer and action, devotion and duty. After the moment of worship and inspiration, it became the time to take the basin and the towel and put faith into action.

Are you aware of the dynamic that is taking place here? *Jesus went straight from the table that is the symbol of his sacrifice for us to the towel and basin that is the symbol of our sacrificial service in his name to others.* He saw nothing incongruous in passing from the solemn breaking of bread and the pouring of wine to the towel and basin, from instituting the sacrament of his body and blood to scrubbing the dirty feet of the disciples. Jesus has left us the symbol of a towel and basin so as to remind us that he came among us as a humble servant, to give his life as a ransom for many. *If "the same mind is in us that is in Christ Jesus," then our lives are committed to practical, humble, and costly service to one another.*

The Cross

The third symbol, the cross, was not chosen by Jesus, but forced upon him by those who sought to destroy him. The cross is the "emblem of suffering and shame." How scandalous that this is the place where the Son of God is to end his life. At the cross on Good Friday, the world thought that it was done with this Jesus of Nazareth. The cross even appeared to his disciples and closest friends as the end of everything.

Hans Kung, the Catholic theologian, points out that anyone who thinks that all religions and their "founders" are alike will see the difference which appears if one compares the death of such men. Buddha died at the age of eighty, peacefully, surrounded by his disciples. Confucius returned in his old age to Lu, spending the last years of his life editing the ancient manuscript writings of his people. Muhammad, after enjoying his last years as political ruler of Arabia, died in the midst of his harem in the arms of his favorite wife. Jesus is a young man of 33, who after a brief span of three years of public ministry is expelled from society. He is forsaken by his disciples, mocked and ridiculed by his opponents, abandoned by his closest friends, even by God. He goes through a ritual of death that is one of the most atrocious and enigmatic ever invented by man's ingenious cruelty. His death is described briefly and with staggering simplicity: "Then Jesus cried again with a loud voice and breathed his last" (Matthew 27:50).

How incredible that Jesus would go from angels announcing his birth from on high to shepherds and wise men, to the time of the Spirit of God descending upon him at the time of his baptism, to the confession of Peter at Caesarea, to Philip confessing to him, "You are Christ, the son of the living God" and to the "Hosannas" from the crowds on Palm Sunday to death on a despised cross erected on a lonely and barren hill called Golgotha, the place of the skull, where he cried alone, "My God, my God, why have you forsaken me?" (Matthew 27:46). The cross is the emblem of God's love and hope for a dying world.

Jesus has left us these three vivid symbols which speak to us of the reality of his life. The cup and the loaf, the towel and the basin, and the cross have a special meaning to us on this Passion Sunday because we are entering Holy Week. This week we will experience the reality of these symbols in a very dramatic way as we participate in Maundy Thursday and Good Friday. May they become for us symbols of hope and reality.

The Friend
Of Sinners

1 Corinthians 11:23-26

Jesus' critics complained that "this fellow welcomes sinners and eats with them" (Luke 15:2). They were upset because this motley crew who did not keep the law and never darkened the door of the synagogue became Jesus' friends. They felt that it was repulsive and repugnant that a man of his stature who claimed to be the Son of God welcomed these sinners and ate with them. These critics were convinced that it was a violation of the nature and purpose of true religion. That begs the question — what is true religion? Here is the message that the church must never forget — that Jesus welcomed sinners and not only welcomed them but also ate with them.

Jesus Is Our Friend

On this Maundy Thursday we are all invited to the table of the Lord. All that Jesus asks of us in coming is that we do this in remembrance of him. What is it that we are to remember? *That Jesus is our friend.* He promises to come to us as we come to the Lord's table. Do you sometimes feel that you have no right to come because your faith is not strong enough or sure enough? Do you feel you have the right to come because you talk about feeding the hungry, caring for the homeless, defending the cause of the poor and oppressed, but you don't do very much?

Sometimes during the celebration of communion do you feel only the absence, when you know it is here, above all places, that you are supposed to feel the presence of God? Do you feel somewhat like an outsider because you do not feel much of anything —

neither an overwhelming feeling of the sense of sinfulness or a spiritual high? Does your mind sometimes wander when you are supposed to be in an attitude of prayer? Do you find yourself looking at your watch and wondering how long it will take to get everyone served so that you can get out in time to beat the Baptists and the Presbyterians to the cafeteria? Then hear this: the Lord's table is for people just like you. You do not have to do anything, be anything, or feel anything to make yourself spiritually, psychologically, or morally worthy to come to the Lord's table. You do not even need to make yourself worthy by telling yourself how unworthy you are.

The host who invites you today to his table is not the friend of only those who are faithful, pious, and good. He is the friend of such sinners and outsiders that you know yourself to be. So if your faith is weak and your doubts are strong, if your motives are questionable and your spirituality leaves something to be desired, if your life will not stand up to careful examination, then you are invited to the Lord's table. You may be surprised to discover as you eat and drink that it is not so much how we come to Christ as how Christ comes to us which makes the reconciling and renewing presence of God real in our lives. On this Maundy Thursday in our Holy Week pilgrimage it is not so much that we reach up from the midst of our despair to where Christ is, but that God through Christ comes to us where we are. Here at the Lord's table we meet Christ at the level of our need. God comes to us where we are, in the eating from a common loaf and drinking from a common cup.

Jesus Is The Friend Of All

Not only is Jesus my friend, but also I need to remember that he is the friend of all those other sinners who come to the Lord's table with me. He is the friend of fellow Christians whose theology is too liberal or too conservative for me. He is the friend of those Christians whose religious experience and faith and life are so different from mine that I wonder if they are Christian at all. He is the friend of those who offend me because they are too pious or not pious enough. He is the friend of those who are too right or too left in their political views or too sexist or racist. He is the friend

52

of all of those around me that I just plain don't like. He is the friend of people I would not invite to dinner at my house, but they are invited to Jesus' table. The fact is, Jesus is their friend also. How can I eat and drink in his company without eating and drinking in their company? If Jesus is not too good to associate with them, how could I ever consider myself as being too good to associate with them? This does not mean that I agree with everything they say or approve of everything they do, but if Jesus is their friend, ought they not also to be my friends? It is possible that we can be reconciled to one another as we eat and drink in the company of one who is the friend of all of us sinners.

Jesus Is The Friend Of Sinners Everywhere

Not only is Jesus my friend, and our friend, but he is everybody's friend. He is the friend of sinners and outsiders everywhere. He is the friend of sinners who are believers and sinners who are unbelievers, right-wing sinners and left-wing sinners, sinners who are oppressed, and sinners who are oppressors. He is the friend of red, yellow, black, and white sinners. We cannot eat or drink with Christ if we do not eat and drink in eager anticipation of the great feast when "Christ comes in final victory and we feast at his heavenly banquet," when all kinds of sinners from the east, west, north, and south will sit together at the table of the Lord.

As we come to God's table we do not need to be afraid of differences anymore, because as Paul reminds us in Ephesians 2, "For Christ is our peace; in his flesh he has made both groups into one and has broken down the dividing wall, that is, the hostility between us " (2:14).

The best news we can hear today is this: "Jesus welcomes sinners." There is hope for you and me. We can come to the Lord's table because we have a friend in Jesus.

53

The Cross Reminds Us Who Jesus Is — Who We Are

Hebrews 10:16-25

The writer of Hebrews has been building up to this moment. This is the climax of his whole presentation. He declares to the people that the curtain shielding the Holy of Holies has been parted and the way to the living God has been opened. We can approach with confidence because the merciful voice of God announces, "I will remember their sins and their lawless deeds no more" (v. 17).

Earlier the writer declared, "Without the shedding of blood there is no forgiveness of sins" (9:22). Jesus, the great High Priest, has made the unblemished offering, the sacrifice of himself on behalf of all and "by a single offering he has perfected for all time those who are sanctified" (10:14). The writer is saying to the congregation that your warfare is ended and your sins are now forgiven because of what Jesus has accomplished as the great High Priest once and for all. It need not be repeated. The sacrifice of Jesus reveals clearly God's love for us. Within his life and teachings the heart of God is revealed for all to see and experience. We can look at the life of Jesus and say, "That is what God is like." Barclay points out that "the life and death of Jesus was an act of perfect obedience and therefore, the only perfect sacrifice" (Barclay, *Hebrews*, p. 117).

The theme of scripture has always been that the only sacrifice God desires is that of love and obedience: "For I desire steadfast love and not sacrifice" (Hosea 6:6). The writer of Hebrews declares that in the life and death of Jesus that is precisely the sacrifice God has received. Perfection cannot be improved upon. In

Jesus there is at one and the same time the perfect revelation of God and the perfect offering of obedience. Jesus' sacrifice cannot and need not ever be made again. Therefore, on this Good Friday it is proper that we focus on the one symbol which seems to gather up all of these aspects regarding the life of Jesus which the writer of Hebrews presents — the *cross* of Jesus.

When Peter made that great confession at Caesarea Philippi, "You are the Messiah," he did not fully comprehend what this meant. And when Jesus responded to his confession, Peter did not understand the significance of Jesus' words. Immediately following Peter's confession Jesus told his disciples that he must go to Jerusalem and suffer, be killed, and on the third day be raised. When Peter took Jesus aside and rebuked him, he seemed to be saying, "This is not what I had in mind. Stop spreading such rumors about death, and the cross, for both your sake and ours. This could get both of us into trouble." Jesus' response was, "If any want to become my followers, let them deny themselves and take up their cross and follow me. For those who want to save their life will lose it, and those who lose their life for my sake will find it" (Matthew 16:24-25). This is not what Peter had in mind regarding the Messiah. His ideas of messiahship were related more to political and military power and accomplishment. At this moment Peter and Jesus were worlds apart. But the cross on Good Friday was the stark reality of the meaning of the words spoken by Jesus at Caesarea Philippi regarding his death, something the disciples failed to comprehend. At Calvary, Peter was seriously reflecting on those words which Jesus had spoken to him.

For the writer of Hebrews, on the cross Jesus, as the Great High Priest, had now made a complete, full, and perfect sacrifice for human sin. But the cross continues to be a "stumbling block" and "foolishness" to many. In John 6, the cross is the dividing line, the line of demarcation, between the true disciples and the hangers-on. In this chapter the cross was beginning to cast its shadow across Jesus' life and "because of this many of his disciples turned back and no longer went about with him" (John 6:66). The cross suggested a demand, a commitment, and to them it was unreasonable and many left. But the demand of the gospel and the cross has never been any less. Today it still demands self-denial, the taking of one's cross and following Christ, and losing one's life for the sake of others and the kingdom of God. Thereby one finds life.

Furthermore, the cross presents us with some understanding, hope, and meaning in the midst of our suffering. The only answer to human suffering is to be found in the cross of Christ. The cross reminds us that in our own loss, tragedy, and pain God has been there before us. There are footprints in the sand. The cross tells us where God is — God is in the midst of human life with all of its pain, anguish, and death. Because of the cross, the God we turn to in our distress is a God with a human face. Gustavo Guttierrez reminds us that Jesus' cry from the cross, "My God, my God, why have you forsaken me?" renders more audible and more penetrating the cries of all who suffer, and the cry of Jesus is the leading voice to which all the voices of those who suffer unjustly are joined (*On Job*, Orbis Books, p. 101). In regard to human suffering and death, it is in the cross of Jesus that God is at work *in* death to bring about life. In this situation God does not work as one who stands on the outside, like some welfare administrator giving out food stamps. God does not view our suffering from a kind of detached objectivity, but God enters through the cross into the mournful situation, working for good from within. In the crucifixion of Jesus, God experiences our suffering from inside. God, through the cross, suffered and died in solidarity with us. Herein is our hope. The God who bids us to come to him has outstretched arms and hands that bear the marks of the nail prints.

The story is told about Charles XII who visited a seaport town in Sweden in 1716. He went to the village church unannounced to worship. When the pastor learned that King Charles was present he wondered whether he should preach the sermon he had prepared or take the opportunity to praise the king for his leadership. He decided to lay aside his sermon. A short time later the church received a special gift from the king. The pastor eagerly called together the entire congregation to share in the opening of the gift. When they opened the large box they discovered a life-size crucifix and attached to it was a note from the king which read, "Let this crucifix stand on the pillar next to the pulpit so that all who stand there will be reminded of their proper subject." In the chancel of nearly every church is a cross. The cross should remind us as a church of the nature and purpose of our task and mission. The cross reminds us that the life of Jesus involved humility, service, sacrifice, and suffering, and these characteristics should denote the life and ministry of the church as well. The cross reminds the preacher who stands in the pulpit of his or her proper subject, which is to "preach Christ crucified." The cross reminds all who come to worship that God so loved the world that God gave his only son for you. The cross reminds all of us, regardless of what happens in our lives, that God loves us and cares for us.

The writer of Hebrews, as is his habit, clinches his argument with a quotation from Scripture. Here in the text he uses a quotation from Jeremiah, "I will remember their sins no more" (Jeremiah 31:34). Because of the cross of Jesus the barrier of sin is forever taken away.

Hear The Good News!

1 Corinthians 15:1-11

Throughout the world today great masses of Christians will gather for worship. Some of these services will begin at dawn. A huge throng will gather at Saint Peter's Square in Rome. Churches in cities, towns, and hamlets across the U.S. will be packed; small country churches are anticipating their highest attendance of the year. The reason — today is Easter. It is Resurrection Day! It is a day to proclaim the good news? What is the good news? It is that "Christ is Risen — He is Risen Indeed!" What does this mean for us? It means that goodness has triumphed over evil, that truth is stronger than falsehood, that light is greater than darkness, and that hope is victorious over despair and disappointment. It means above all that life has conquered death. The apostle Paul reminds us in 1 Corinthians 15:26 that the last enemy — death — has been destroyed. Easter's good news means that "we who have borne the image of the dust will also bear the image of the man of heaven" (v. 49). Easter brings to us a transformation from the "perishable to the imperishable" (v. 42), from "dishonor to glory," from "weakness to power" (v. 43), and this mortal body will put on immortality (v. 53b). Today, the apostle bids all Christians around the world who make up the *holy catholic Church* to raise their many voices and join in the chorus: "Death has been swallowed up in victory ... thanks be to God, who gives us the victory through our Lord Jesus Christ" (vv. 54b, 57).

I come today with the same responsibility the apostle felt in writing 1 Corinthians 15, to "remind you, brothers and sisters, of the good news" (v. 1a). On this Resurrection Day the good news is "that Christ died for our sins ... that he was buried ... he was raised on the third day" (vv. 3b-4). We have come that we may proclaim our heartfelt praise and gratitude, saying with the apostle, "Thanks be to God, who gives us the victory through our Lord Jesus Christ" (v. 57).

Jesus Died For Our Sins

Late on Friday afternoon darkness fell across Calvary and Jesus uttered a loud cry and breathed his last. Charles Wesley wrote, "The immortal God for me hath died; My Lord, my Love is crucified."

Jesus entered into a world saturated with violence. A world where the poor were neglected, women beaten and raped, children abused, the earth plundered, and the prophets were murdered so that the order of society and the world would not be disturbed. Daniel Migliore points out that when Jesus disturbs that order — announces God's forgiveness of sinners, promises the future to the poor, welcomes outcasts and strangers, calls all to repentance and a new way of life characterized by love of God and others — when Jesus does this, it should be no surprise that Jesus must suffer at the hands of such a world built upon hostility and violence. "Jesus became the victim of violence because he threatened the world of violence" (Daniel Migliore, *Faith Seeking Understanding*, 1991, p. 159).

Jesus lived and died for all of us. Migliore declares that "Jesus was raised on a cross before the world as the chief cornerstone of a new humanity that no longer espouses the way of violence and no longer wills to live at the expense of victims." He points out how the death of Jesus impinges upon the first century world as well as our world. First, Christ died for us in order to expose our world of violence for what it is — a world that stands under the judgment of God. Second, the cross of Christ is God's own gift of costly love, mediating God's forgiveness and friendship in the midst of a violent world. By freely taking up the cross, God in Christ forgives sinners and enters into solidarity with all the wretched of the earth. Third, the cross of Christ etches deeply into human history the truth that God's compassion is greater than the murderous passions of the world, "that God's free forgiveness is greater than our paralyzing recognition of guilt, that God's way of life is greater than our way of death" (Migliore, *ibid.*, p. 160f).

As the evening shadows on Good Friday began to close around the cross where the limp and lifeless body of Jesus hung, the disciples long before this hour had fled and were in hiding. The women who had watched from a distance now departed. The New Testament scholar Raymond Brown points out, "Like the prophet Jeremiah, Jesus was seen as a disturber of the religious structure. Were Jesus to appear in our day he would probably be arrested and tried again. Most of those finding him guilty would identify themselves as Christians and think they were rejecting an impostor" (*Newsweek*, April 4, 1991, p. 48f).

Jesus Was Buried

When evening came Joseph of Arimathea, a respected member of the Sanhedrin Council, took courage and went to Pilate and asked for the body of Jesus so that he might give it a proper burial. Pilate wondered if Jesus was dead, and being informed by a centurion that he was indeed dead, he permitted Joseph to take the body. So Joseph took the body and wrapped it in a clean linen cloth and laid it in his own tomb. He placed a large stone in front of the tomb and departed. It has been said that Joseph gave Jesus a tomb after he was dead, but did not support him during his life. However, Barclay points out that Joseph displayed the greatest courage of all. He came out to support a crucified criminal, and he braved the resentment of Pilate, as well as the hatred and resentment of the Jews (Barclay, *Matthew*, vol. 2, p. 412). He did everything that was possible for him to do. Matthew tells us that Mary Magdalene and the other Mary were there, sitting next to the tomb, observing what Joseph had done.

The dawn came — it was Saturday, the Sabbath. It was a quiet day. Such a contrast to the day before. Worship was held in the temple as usual. For many it was a normal Sabbath day. Men stood around the temple following the worship in small groups, discussing the events of the day before. They nodded their heads approvingly, saying to one another, "Men did what they had to do," and that was the end of that. They each departed to their own homes, convinced that this "Jesus of Nazareth thing" was finally over. Saturday came and went — it was uneventful. Jesus' body was in the tomb and his disciples were in hiding.

Jesus Was Raised On The Third Day

It was not lawful to prepare a body for burial on the Sabbath. So when the Sabbath was past, on the first day of the week, the women ventured out early in the morning for the cemetery where Jesus was buried. It was dark and cold as they made their way through the streets of Jerusalem. The streets were calm, in stark contrast to Friday's orgy of violence and crucifixion. They risked much as they approached the tomb which was guarded by soldiers who were hostile to their cause. The Gospels all agree that the women were the only disciples left. After Good Friday everyone else was in hiding. So in this dark early morning hour prior to the sunrise these three women with aching hearts made their way to the tomb to perform a final act of devotion for their departed Lord.

What occupied their minds as they made their way to the tomb was not the danger that their journey entailed, but how they were going to remove the large stone that blocked the entrance to the tomb. As they traveled to the tomb they said to one another, "Who will roll away the stone for us from the entrance of the tomb?" (Mark 16:3). Why is it that we tend to face the difficult situations in our lives as though only mundane, human forces are at work within our lives? It is interesting how the rock got there in the first place. Joseph of Arimathea had placed it there. But Pilate sent soldiers to guard the tomb as a measure to secure it against robbery lest the disciples come and take away the body and then declare that he had risen (Matthew 27:62-66). So Pilate took this precautionary measure to keep this from happening. Frederick Buechner states that in trying to prevent the resurrection from happening Pilate sent a few soldiers to keep the stone in place. Buechner suggests that this is "like trying to stop the wind with a machine gun ... How does an old man (Pilate) keep the sun from shining? How do soldiers secure the world against a miracle?" (Buechner, *The Magnificent Defeat,* p. 77).

But the women were distraught about the stone which they thought stood between them and their act of devotion and respect. Their worry and frustration was the result of realizing that they did not have the physical strength to remove the stone. It was beyond them. But they failed to realize that "something beyond them" was already at work in their lives. Often we face obstacles and barriers in our lives and the question is asked, "When will this stone be rolled away?" The answer is obvious: Never! Never, as long as we think only in terms of our human strength. How easily our pain, loss, sorrow, or disappointment often captures all of our attention to the point that we lose sight of the presence and power of the risen Christ. When obstacles and barriers stand in our way we need to stop and ask ourselves, "Where is faith and prayer in all of this?" The women hurried and worried on their way to the tomb. Like many of us there was an obstacle, a barrier in their lives, frustrating their plans and ambitions — they did not know how to handle it.

The women on that first Easter morning whose heavy hearts were burdened with feelings of both disappointment and inadequacy made a remarkable discovery as they approached the tomb — God was there ahead of them — the rock had been removed and Christ was risen! The unexpected had occurred. They came to the tomb expecting what one usually finds in the aftermath of a crucifixion — a dead body. They came prepared to anoint the body and prepare it for burial. They came expecting to deal with death, defeat, and despair. They came expecting death and discovered life. Easter reminds us that God changes the despair, defeat, and darkness of Good Friday into the hope and life of Easter. On Good Friday the world said, "No!" to the life of Jesus, but on Easter morning God said an eternal, "Yes!"

James Masefield in his poem, "The Widow on Bye Street," depicts a scene of dramatic agony. A young man is about to be executed for crimes against the state. In the crowd witnessing the events is his widowed mother, who is about to be left all alone in the world. As the trap door beneath the son's feet is opened, his mother crumbles to the ground and cries, "Things are broken — too broken to mend." Part of her anguish had to do with her past, her sense of failure as a parent. Part had to do with the future, her utter sense of hopelessness, feeling that her very existence was broken beyond repair. Today many feel that things are too broken to mend — health, hopes, careers, and relationships. The future is as dreary as it was for those women on their way to the tomb on the first Easter morning, strewn with barriers which appear like gravestones that are too heavy and seem impossible to remove. Brokenness is the reality of human life — broken homes, broken hearts, broken hopes, and broken lives. The good news of Easter Sunday is that God is there ahead of you — Christ is risen. Death is conquered. There is enough power in God's love and grace to deal with whatever brokenness we may be experiencing. The resurrection of Jesus trumpets today an incredible truth — whoever you are, whatever your pain, problems, anxiety, affliction, frustration, or failures — you need not despair. God is there ahead of you preparing and leading the way.

I am certain that at some point you have asked the question, "Does anyone care?" Families care most of the time and friends care some of the time, but God cares all of the time. Jesus is the great mender of broken things. He began mending ploughs in his father's carpenter shop in Nazareth, and he went on to mend men and women who were broken in body, mind, and spirit. Today Jesus seeks to mend not only broken lives, but also a broken world. The resurrected, living Christ is there ahead of you in your brokenness preparing the way to togetherness, wholeness, and healing. Charles Wesley has said it so well:

> *He speaks and listening to his voice,*
> *new life the dead receive.*
>
> *The mournful, broken hearts rejoice,*
> *the humble poor believe.*

64

Pass
It On

1 John 1:1—2:2

James Stewart tells the story of two men who had been business partners for over twenty years who met one Sunday morning as they were leaving a restaurant. One of them asked, "Where are you going this morning?" "I am going to play golf, what about you?" he replied. Responding rather apologetically he said, " I am going to church." The other man said, "Why don't you give up that church stuff?" The man replied, "What do you mean?" "Well," he answered, "we have been business partners for twenty years. We have worked together, attended board meetings together, and lunched together, and in all of these twenty years you have never talked to me about going to church with you. Obviously, it doesn't mean that much to you." The logic of this story is irresistible. If Christ is the joy of life and through your contact with him you have a new experience of wonder and light, so that the old, gray, monotonous world has given way to a life of joy, peace, power, and a love for others, then surely you should long to pass it on.

These Sundays following Easter provide us with an opportunity to reflect upon what it means to witness to the resurrection in our day-to-day lives. Resurrection can seem like a remote, otherworldly event that has nothing to do with the mundane realities of our relationships. The challenge for us is to discover how we can communicate the resurrection as a daily reality in our lives. Whenever we experience new life, when life is reborn and love and faith are rekindled, we experience resurrection. When we recognize these experiences as resurrection moments, we then can be witnesses to them. To be witnesses to the resurrection is at the very heart of our ministry to one another.

In 1 John 1, the writer says to his readers that he wants to declare to them what he has heard, what he has seen with his eyes and touched with his own hands "concerning the word of life." He said, "We declare to you what we have seen and heard so that you also may have fellowship with us and truly our fellowship is with the Father and with his Son Jesus Christ" (v. 3). Notice that John talks about *hearing, seeing, touching* — these are the marks of authentic religion, a religious experience that the writer was anxious to share.

To share one's faith is to enrich one's faith. I enjoy raising flowers. I have discovered through the years that it is important to plant the right flowers at the right time in the right place. For the hot, dry summer months it is important to select the right flowers that can withstand the hot summer sun and the dry conditions of central Florida. One flower that does well in the summer is the zinnia. It thrives in the hot summer and it provides a magnificent array of beautiful colors. There is one variety of zinnia that is called "Cut and Come Again." It is well named. When one flower is cut, three are ready to take its place. The more you cut and give away the more you have. This is exactly what happens when you share your faith. The more you give away the more you have. God has given you this treasure to share, and by sharing your faith your faith is enriched.

We need to remember that Methodism began as a lay movement. For Wesley, preaching and testifying belonged to the whole church. At the beginning of the Wesleyan revival laypeople were utilized to spread the gospel. Wesley felt it was a fatal mistake to leave the task of spreading the gospel to the ordained clergy. He felt it was heresy to turn the ministry of the Christian Church into a clergy-dominated religion. Across the world today, church growth is the greatest where the laity are the most involved. The small group movement, which is lay-centered like early Methodism, is putting vitality, vision, and enthusiasm back into our church.

Leslie Weatherhead, the English pastor and psychologist, told about a young brilliant doctor he met in London who was working on a number of experiments in a laboratory that was attached to the university. He was doing cancer research and his work was supported by some of the most distinguished scientists in London. Weatherhead said that he watched him work in a small, ill-ventilated room in the basement of the university. The doctor told Weatherhead that if these experiments turned out as successfully as he had every right to hope they would, then he would have a new way of treating this particular cancer with some hope of recovery for the patient. Weatherhead asked him, "What will you then do?" With a glow on his face, with enthusiasm in his voice and a shining in his eyes, he exclaimed, "I shall tell the world." We have come to worship with great expectations. With a glow on our faces, enthusiasm in our voices, we too have made a discovery — that Jesus Christ is Lord and he is among his people. Christ has come to set the captive free. "He breaks the power of cancelled sin. He sets the prisoner free!" What then? We leave to tell the world, to share our discovery, and to pass it on.

In the study of the Book of Acts, the one underlying purpose that reappears over and over again during the early Church's formation is the encouragement to be a witness to the resurrection. The key verse to the entire book is 1:8: "But you will receive power when the Holy Spirit has come upon you; and you will be my witnesses in Jerusalem, in all of Judea and Samaria, and to the ends of the earth." The following 28 chapters in Acts tell the story of the results of that witness. What had started in the first two chapters, by chapter 28 had spread all the way to Rome, the very center of power and authority. When Peter completed his great sermon at Pentecost, he made this final statement: "This Jesus God raised up, and of that all of us are witnesses" (Acts 2:32). Our New Testament faith is a witnessing faith. D. T. Niles, the bishop of Sri Lanka, defined our witnessing as "one beggar telling another beggar where to find bread."

The Bible teaches us that the "word became flesh." For the word of God to be communicated, it must become flesh. Phillips Brooks, the great New England preacher of a century ago, maintained that "truth is expressed through personality." Personality is the vehicle for conveying God's truth. Our task is to spread the good news of God's story in light of our own particular story, with the hope that people will respond in faith. The telling of God's story through our own story expresses God's truth and love through human experience that is identifiable to all who hear it. It is through the lives of real people that we see and hear the story of God's redeeming grace. There was a little girl who had a brief line in a Sunday school Christmas program. All she had to say was, "I am the light of the world." She rehearsed it until she knew it. The night of the program arrived and the little girl was confident, but her mother was nervous. When the little girl saw all of the people at the program, she became frightened and forgot her words. She twisted and turned her eyes towards the ceiling, but for the life of her, she could not remember her line. Her mother tried to prompt her from offstage. Carefully and slowly the mother's lips formed the words, "I am the light of the world." The little girl straightened and with a deep breath and loud voice announced, "My mother is the light of the world." In a real sense, so are we all.

We are all called to be disciples. The word "disciple" denotes a call, a commitment (a response to the call) and a discipline (the assuming of a lifestyle). Dietrich Bonhoeffer in his book, *The Cost of Discipleship,* reminds us that discipleship has a cost; it comes with a price tag. How could we ever be a disciple, enter discipleship without discipline? He defines "cheap grace" as seeking discipleship without discipline, faith without commitment, communion without confession, and baptism without repentance. "Cheap grace" produces a Christian witness that is weak and ineffective.

Ron Fraser, who was the baseball coach at the University of Miami, was one of the most successful college baseball coaches of all time. He had numerous opportunities to manage in the major leagues, but he remained at Miami where he established an outstanding record. When asked why he was so successful as a baseball coach, his answer was simply, "I teach my players the fundamentals over and over and over again." For Fraser, the fundamentals were pitching, fielding, and running the bases. His record speaks for itself.

Successful Christian discipleship is mastering the basics. John Wesley brought renewal to the Church of England in the eighteenth century by getting back to the basics. The Church of England had lost sight of the basics of the Christian life and thus became cold and lifeless. Wesley established the class meeting, a small group meeting that followed three basic principles: prayer, study of the scriptures, and witnessing. Every renewal of the Church from then to now has come through the same process. This has become the basis for the phenomenal success of the Church in Africa and in Korea today. For us today, the success of the Christian life will always contain these basic elements: prayer, study, and witness.

Eight-year-old Benny died of AIDS in 1987. CBS made a movie drama about the trauma called *Moving Toward the Light*. As Benny lies dying in his mother's arms, he asks, "What will it be like?" His mother whispers softly into his ear: "You will see a light, Benny, far away — a beautiful, shining light at the end of a long tunnel. And your spirit will lift you out of your body and start to travel toward the light. And as you go, a veil will be lifted from your eyes, and suddenly, you will see everything ... But most of all, you will feel a tremendous sense of love." "Will it take long?" Benny asks. "No," his mother answers, "Not long at all. Like the twinkling of an eye."

"This is the message we have heard from him and proclaim to you, that God is light and in him is no darkness at all" (1 John 1:5).

Go and pass it on!

Heaven
And Hope

1 John 3:1-7

The theme of 1 John all along has been the love of God. The author now expands that love in the phrase, "the children of God," and for the first time he considers what it means to be the children of God. Earlier, he presented love within the fellowship and now he speaks of the meaning of God's love for us and its implications for the future. The consequences and proof of the love of God are evident in being called "the children of God." He is careful to point out that the love of God is a gift; we do not earn it.

Our text in verses 2 and 3 reflects both the certainty and the sobriety of Christian expectation with regard to the conditions of life to come, as well as its moral implications. The moral and ethical implications of being the children of God are reflected in John's words in 2:6, we "ought to walk just as he walked."

One scholar has pointed out that the uncertainty implied by our not knowing what we shall be (v. 2) is more than offset by the assurance that we are already "now" the children of God (D. Moody Smith, *Interpretation Commentary*, 1-2-3 John, p. 77f). John asserts that it is safe to assume that we shall be something better rather than worse. Even in the face of uncertainty ("what we will be has not yet been revealed"), the believer is in a state of hopeful expectation, for "we shall see him as he is." The question is: Have Christians seen Jesus as he is? The disciples saw the earthly Jesus, this is possibly true for John, but they really never saw Jesus as he was or is (Smith, *ibid.,* p. 78). Their post-resurrection knowledge of him revealed how little they really knew him. Most believers

71

have not seen Jesus at all (John 20:29). The promise to "see him as he is" is both relevant and hopeful, especially when accompanied by the assurance that "we shall be like him." In a sense, verse 3 is a reaffirming of Jesus' promise to his disciples in John 17:24, that they will be with him in heaven to witness to the glory that Jesus had prior to creation. There are two themes that stand out quite clearly in our text: Heaven and Hope.

What Will Heaven Be Like?

How many times have you been asked or asked yourself, "What will heaven be like?" For centuries Christians have sought to answer that question, especially after the death of a spouse, a family member, or a loved one. After all of our inquiry, what do we really know about heaven, and does it really matter? We stand week after week and affirm, "I believe in the resurrection of the body and life everlasting." What do you think about as you repeat those words? Do you repeat them with the conviction that you know there is a real heaven to which you are headed? Much of the Church's evangelism is based on this very assumption, when unbelievers are asked, "If you die this very day, do you know you will go to heaven?" Do you repeat this part of the creed with firm conviction that there is a real heaven, or do you go along with this part of the creed although it is not really that important to your theology or faith?

David H. C. Read has pointed out that there is a popular notion that the Bible is a book about heaven and the Christian, who is headed in that direction, can find a great deal of detail in the scriptures regarding heaven's nature and character. If you turn to the Bible for information regarding the next world, you will be disappointed (David H. C. Read, *Expository Times*, September 1978, p. 370). Jesus took it for granted that we are headed for new life beyond the grave, yet he discouraged any inquisitiveness regarding its nature. To talk about the furniture of heaven or the temperature of hell is mere speculation. The best that the apostle Paul could do was to come up with the thought that we would have a "spiritual body" (1 Corinthians 15). This sounds like a contradiction in

72

terms, but it is actually a shield against crude ideas of our present physical bodies being reconstituted in a future life.

Here in 1 John the author is writing to a Christian congregation which is as diverse in saintliness and sinfulness as our congregations, but they are united in their commitment to Jesus Christ. He reminds the congregation, "We are the children of God now," (v. 2a) and God does not let his children drift into oblivion when the body dies. On numerous occasions Jesus reminded his disciples that God is God, not of the dead, but of the living — for in him all are in fact alive, "Because I live, you also will live" (John 14:19b). We know nothing about heaven, except for these words of John: "What we do know is this: when he is revealed, we will be like him, for we will see him as he is" (v. 2b). In these words there is no hesitancy, no agnosticism, no doubt or perhaps, but we know "we will be like him." The truth that emerges is "that heaven is to be thought of in terms of our growth into the image of God in the likeness of Jesus Christ — in his delight in the Father's glory, his overflowing love for every creature, his joy of human companionship, his sense of beauty and mystery, his passion for justice, his vision for peace, and above all his purity of heart" (Read, *ibid.*). It is the pure of heart who shall see God — that is what heaven is like.

Purified By Hope

John points out in verse 4, "And all who have this hope in him purify themselves." Those who enter into this hope seek to be pure, as Christ is pure. In other words, this conviction about heaven should be a moral power in our lives right now. It is this hope that sets the whole course of our lives. This hope purifies. It is a hope that brings a sense of direction for an ambiguous future. There are many things these Christians do not understand, but they do know "that when Christ is revealed, they will be like him, for they shall see him as he is." This hope purifies against hopelessness and despair.

This hope was important for first century Christians, because there was so little of it in the world around them. As the Christians in the first two centuries began to leave the Jewish community and venture into the Gentile world, it was a bleak world indeed. It was a world that was deeply influenced by the Stoics and the Greek gods. History for the Gentiles was cyclical — constantly repeating itself in the same harsh and cruel events. The future in such a world was bleak and hopeless. It was a superstitious world controlled by blind fate. The vices of the gods became the virtues of men and women pulling society down to the depths of human despair and immorality. The apostle Paul gives an accurate account of the Gentile world in Ephesians 2:12: "Remember that you were at that time without Christ, being aliens from the commonwealth of Israel, and strangers to the covenant of promise, having no hope and without Christ in the world."

What a contrast the text is in regard to the world in which these first-century Christians were living. John's words in 3:1 reminded them that they were "called children of God," giving them a sense of destiny and hope. For these early Christians living in a dark and superstitious world controlled by a blind fate, these words provided direction and purpose. Not only were they called to be the children of God, but the time would come when their Lord would be revealed and they would see him as he is. This provided for them a sense of history that was both optimistic and hopeful. History was important to these Christians because God had chosen them to be his children. Life was meaningful and purposeful because it was based on the promise of God. They felt themselves to be a people of destiny and direction. Therefore, this hope purified them from the despair and superstition that was so prevalent in the world around them.

The hope of heaven is a purifying hope for us as well. For us it is a symbol of the consummated reign of God bringing everlasting life in the depth of fellowship with God through Jesus Christ. Eternal life is unbroken and unending communion, the sharing of life with others in the God whose being is in community. We need to recognize the fact that the biblical images of eternal life are profoundly communal — expressed as the kingdom of God, the great banquet, the new Jerusalem coming down from heaven. Eternal life is no endless extension of the existence of isolated selves, no perpetuation of individualism and infinity. "Eternal life means the unending participation in God's eternal community of love. Such life in communion with others is not the loss but the fulfillment of personal identity in relationship with God and others" (Migliore, *Faith Seeking Understanding*, p. 246). This purifying hope of the everlasting life of God is inexhaustibly rich. We will never be bored by it or ever feel that we have gotten to the bottom of it. In everlasting praise of God there will be new surprises and adventures as God's gift of life and love goes on unfolding itself boundlessly.

Our hope is grounded in the reality of God who transcends death and in whose love we continue to know and be known. It is this hope that purifies us against despair and futility. James L. Kidd tells the story about the time that his mother-in-law died, and his wife had a wonderful dream. Her father and their oldest son had died a few years before, and when her mother arrived in heaven she found them playing a game of chess as they often did when alive. She stood beside them, but at first they ignored her because they were so engrossed in their game. Her son Bruce, who still appeared to be thirteen, noticed his grandmother. So he set aside the chess board, pulled out a deck of cards, and dealt her in. Kidd concluded by saying that our hope is that when this life is over we have "a building of God not made with hands that is eternal in the heavens," and when we get there, someone will deal us in.

How many times we are called to face the unknown. It could be a new job, a marriage, a bereavement, or a very difficult decision. It is then that we desire the presence of someone we love and trust. But there are times, and death is one, when no human companion can go with us. It is the presence of Christ and his promise "where I am there you will be also" that provides for us the hope and the courage for the journey.

75

Making
Love Visible

1 John 3:16-24

How do you like being addressed as "little children"? Many times the way a speaker addresses his audience is a clue of what is coming. "Ladies and gentlemen" gives one the feeling that a formal speech is coming. "Friends" is a signal of a different kind of speech, maybe a bit more folksy and intimate. "Brethren" is a sign, especially when women are present, that we are about to hear some sort of sermon that may be out of touch with reality. The apostle addresses us as "little children" and then he appeals to our mature judgment. These words express a certain tenderness and affection, as a father would have for his children. He is reminding us of Jesus' words when he said that it is as little children that we enter the kingdom of God. He is going to talk about the greatest theme in the world — the God who is and the kind of people we are meant to be. He is going to deal with the very heart and center of the Christian life.

God Is Love

"God is love." John is the only writer in the whole Bible who said it. This is the central theme of our Christian faith. The same writer who tells us that God is love is the one who wrote that "God so loved the world that he gave his only Son" (John 3:16a). There are many religions that have something to say about this love, but there is only one that says that this love became visible in the life and death of a human being who was the perfect reflection of the Father in heaven. John begins this epistle by declaring how this love became visible: "We declare to you what was from the beginning, what we have heard, what we have seen with our eyes, what we have looked at and touched with our hands, concerning the word of life — this life was revealed, and we have seen it and testify to it ..." (1:1-2a). John declares that this love of God was made visible in Jesus Christ. Yes, visible. Love became visible as Jesus walked the village streets preaching good news to the poor; visible in the healing of lepers; visible in the casting out of demons; visible in feeding the hungry; visible in his acceptance of the outcast and the downtrodden. This visibility reached its climax in the most vivid manner — the champion of the poor, the friend of sinners, the giver of life is crucified on Calvary. The love of God through Jesus Christ became visible. It was only after John looked back upon the life of Jesus that was lived out so visibly before him that he could say, "God is love."

From Creed To Deed

Today, Christ is gone physically. Now it is only through the Christian that the love of God becomes visible. Our words and our creeds need to be transformed into deeds as John declares in the text, "Let us love, not in words or speech, but in truth and action." A junior high student in reading *King Lear* discovers that she is having difficulty in really encountering King Lear. She is reading the words, but *King Lear* is not meant to be read as much as it is to be acted out — it is a play. The Christian faith is just that way. You have seen the books on major Christian beliefs and what Christians believe. The implications may be that the Christian faith is a set of intellectual propositions. But Jesus was not a philosopher. He did not ask people to agree with him but to follow him. Maybe we are being misled by the way we worship on Sunday morning. What do we do when we come to church? We sit and listen. The pastor talks and we listen. The choir sings and we listen. Do we give the wrong impression about the Christian faith, that it is more of a passion than an action? The fact is, the Christian faith is only known by its performance. The evidence of the Christian faith will always be the Christ-like lives it produces. A secular second century historian declared: "What lives these Christians produce."

That has always been the essence of the Christian faith — making love visible.

Leonard Sweet, Dean of Drew Theological Seminary, tells the story about a woman who is the lay leader of her church in North Carolina. He said she would hardly qualify for a popular definition of a saint. Her methods were unorthodox, her theology was never very apparent, and her language was sprinkled with words that she never learned in Sunday school. But she knew about the world and she had the odd notion that God expected her to be busy in the world on God's behalf.

One day as she cruised down the main street in her hometown, a local policeman stopped a car driven by a youth who was traveling in front of her. She had read in the local paper how the town was supported in part by fines of youthful, out-of-town tourists. She stopped her car behind that of the policeman. "Can I help you, Miss Peggy?" he asked. "Yes, why did you stop that car?" she responded. The officer answered, "I stopped him because he is speeding, and really, it is none of your business." "Well, I am making it my business," she said. "I am sick and tired of you people busting these kids for minor offenses. If he was speeding, then I was speeding. I was traveling behind him at the same speed. You stopped him because he is young, black, and out of state." Irritated, the officer said to her, "This is none of your concern or business." She answered, "I told you it is my business. It is not right and you know it. Let's all go down to the station and talk this over." The policeman did not answer. He got into his car and drove off, muttering to himself something about a "smart-mouth woman." As the woman started her car she said to the young man, "Son, be careful," and drove off. Maybe she had heard a sermon on Sunday about justice and fair play. Here she had an opportunity to speak against an action that she thought was unfair and unjust. She heard Jesus say, "Go and do likewise."

From Belief To Action

In a recent eight-part series on PBS documenting the development of the American West, there was a vivid description of the horrible plight of the Native Americans. Their suffering was beyond description. The massacre, pain, anguish, and suffering of tens of thousands of Native Americans was clearly documented. As has happened in similar incidents, some of the atrocities were done in the name of God. I could not help asking myself while viewing these emotional and soul-wrenching accounts of human death and suffering, "Where was the Christian church?" But that was long ago and far away. But what about our community when the golf courses had signs which read: Gentiles Only. What about signs on rest rooms, water fountains, classrooms, and restaurants that read: White Only. What about invisible signs that still are on many boardrooms and committee rooms that read: Men Only. Where is the voice of the Church today? Our voice is weak and barely a whisper, because we have been partially responsible for erecting the signs in the first place. However, we in the Church are responsible for the signs that hang on certain pulpits that read: Men Only. When in the assembly of the congregation we are challenged by the words of Micah "to do justice, and to love kindness, and to walk humbly with your God" (Micah 6:8) and then confronted with Jesus' words "to love your neighbor," how does that live itself out on Monday mornings? How are you doing in taking the high sounding words of Christian love and concern and turning them into human action? In our text we are to love as Christ loved, "not in words or speech, but in truth and action."

Having Compassion

In Matthew 14 a very interesting event took place in Jesus' life. Jesus traveled by boat to a deserted place in order to get some very needed peace and quiet. The people heard where he was headed, so they traveled by land and got there ahead of him so that when Jesus came ashore, in what he thought was a deserted, quiet place, he was confronted by a great crowd. Jesus' response in seeing the crowd might have been one of consternation. He might have been irritated at their constant demands and being jostled by their presence. He might have easily resented the crowd that was depriving him of a quietness that he so desperately needed after hearing about John the Baptist's death. But it was not to be. He was far from ever finding the crowd a nuisance,

80

instead "he had compassion for them" (v. 14). Why did he draw such a crowd — because a loving, caring, generous person always draws a crowd. Jesus showed his compassion for them by feeding the hungry, healing the sick, casting out demons, comforting the sorrowful, befriending the outcast, and preaching the good news of God's love to the poor.

A loving, caring, and generous Church always draws a crowd. People do not come to church because of what we say, but because of what we do. People do not come because of words and speech, but they come because of truth and action. A non-growing church needs to ask itself if it has a genuine, all-consuming passion and concern for people. It could be that the church is not making a difference in people's lives. So why should they come and support it? They have better places to go and more important things to do. How easy it is to lose a passion for souls. Before a congregation realizes it, proper polity and procedure become more important than people, maintenance and preservation of buildings crowd out opportunities for ministry and the care of souls, and soon such a church finds itself interested in just a select group of people, mainly those just like themselves. Jesus drew a crowd because he loved the people. The church will draw a crowd if it has compassion and love for the people — all people.

I recently returned from West Africa, where I was a visiting lecturer at Trinity Theological College in Legon, Ghana. I met numerous young adults from the United States who were serving in the Peace Corps. One day at the American Club in Accra I met a young woman who was an agriculturalist from the University of Minnesota. She had spent the last two years in Ho, which is a very remote agricultural region in northwest Ghana. In our conversation I discovered she had been working with the Ghanaian farmers in developing new crops, and she was going home for a few months. She looked tired and somewhat haggard. She told me how isolated it had been living in the Ho region and that she had been sick on numerous occasions and had suffered through malaria. She told me after her brief visit to the States that she was coming back to complete her three-year term. I asked her, "Why do you do it? Why do you give up your career back home to go to such a remote area and work under such extremely difficult conditions?" Her answer was simply, "Because I love the people." There is no more noble reason. Barbra Streisand's lyrics are right on target, "People who love people are the happiest people in the world."

The apostle is saying to us in our text to make the love of God visible. I am amazed at the number of people who never get around to doing the things they say are important. We are so busy trying to sound good, look good, and feel good that we never actually have time to do good. The challenge of the text is unmistakable — *let us love, not in word or speech, but in **truth** and **action**.*

Love's Expectations

1 John 4:7-21

Our text expresses the heart of the Gospel: God's love for the world is revealed in the life of Jesus, and those who proclaim that they belong to Jesus seek to love as he loved. God's love was not abstract, but made visible in Jesus, and the author admonishes us to make our love visible rather than sentimental and abstract. Love becomes authentic when it is acted out in the world in concrete ways with others. Philip Halle in his book, *Lest Innocent Blood Be Shed,* reveals an incident in World War II where love became visible in the French village of Le Chambon in 1944. Le Chambon was a farming community of about 5,000 French Protestants. The village carried out the heroic rescue of 5,000 Jews without any betrayal or loss of life. They were inspired and led by the Protestant pastor, Andre Tracome, who called them to fight the Nazis with the "weapons of the Spirit." In doing so they risked their very lives. If caught by the Nazis they would have been put to death. A documentary film was made about this story by a French filmmaker, Pierre Sauvdage, a French Jew who was born in Le Chambon in 1944. What a remarkable demonstration of love.

Scholars feel that this paragraph of scripture (vv. 7-12) is one of the most eloquent statements about love in all of the Johannine literature, if not the entire New Testament. It may not be as well known as 1 Corinthians 13, but it is a more adequate theological discussion about the origin of love than Paul's famous passage. In contrast to Paul's more popular poem, the writer of 1 John gives a distinctively Christian explanation of the origin of love "becoming a more classical model for theology and ethics" (Smith, *Interpretation on Commentary,* p. 106).

The writer declares that love is of God and it is the basic premise of Christian faith, theology, and practice. A failure to love invalidates any claim to know God: "for those who do not love a brother or sister whom they have seen, cannot love God whom they have not seen ... those who love God must love their brothers and sisters also" (vv. 20-21). Is it possible he is making a declaration regarding love because of a situation he has encountered? The author is careful to point out that his statement regarding love is not to be taken out of context. It is to be understood on the basis of God's love as revealed in Jesus. In verses 9-10a, he states that "God's love was revealed among us in this way: God sent his only Son into the world so that we might live through him ... in this is love." Therefore, God defines the nature of love by giving his Son and we, by this love, are to give ourselves to others.

God Takes The Initiative

The author's definition of love begins with the clear assumption that God has taken the initiative. Love results from God's giving up his Son and sending him, as first expressed in John 3:16 along with the parallel passage here in verse 9: "God's love was revealed among us in this way: God sent his only Son into the world so that we might live through him." It is a particularly important factor for John that this love is initiated and proceeds from God: "not that we loved God but that he loved us" (v. 10). Love is not abstract, but is based upon God's concrete, historical deed in the appearance and death of Jesus. This is the heart of the gospel: that God has revealed his love for the world through Jesus and those who declare that they belong to Jesus seek to love as he loved. It has been pointed out that God is accessible to us only as we love. In both the believer as well as God's historic revelation in Jesus, God's reality manifests itself as love (Smith, *ibid.,* p. 108). The writer of 1 John's theme is that apart from love it is meaningless to inquire about God's reality or being, for "God is love, and those who abide in love abide in God" (v. 16b).

No other New Testament writer has spoken so directly and eloquently about the origin and expectations of love as the author of 1 John. Here are both the theological basis and the moral implications of Christian love. Because God loves, we ought to love, not only God, but also one another. Possibly these words were directed to certain members of the church that the author had in mind, but they need to be directed to all members of the Christian community. These words regarding love provide for the Christian Church today the fundamental premise for Christian ethics. God's love is no abstraction, but consists in the giving up of his Son, so the believer's love is not merely an emotion or attitude, but consists of meaningful deeds. Apart from such deeds, the very claim of love becomes empty. We need to ask ourselves: What does this understanding of love mean for us? What does Christian love expect of us in today's world? How do we move from our abstract generalizations and comments about love and loving to incarnating Christian love in our everyday human encounters?

Barriers To Love

The message of the text is clear: We are loved by God and we are to love one another. But the truth is we do not find it easy to love. We are more aware of our fear and pain in relation to others than we are of compassion and connectedness. Living with others can be hell. We see and hear this every day in the media. Love brings both pain and joy, but pain seems to prevail. As we confront the barriers to love, is it possible for us to use them as opportunities for us to grow in grace? If love is genuine, it will always encounter barriers, conflicts, and resistance. Consider those unhappy encounters you have had with spouses, children, neighbors, colleagues, and church members. Do you think, by God's grace, that these encounters could become creative events in your life and that the Spirit can help you to grow in your ability to love?

What do we do when we encounter these barriers to love? I have found some suggestions by Gregory J. Johanson which have proved helpful. He suggests that we recognize a barrier to love, which is usually obvious by our anger, unhappiness, and fear. We need to take responsibility for our part in the barrier, which is the most difficult thing for us to do. We need to invite the Holy Spirit to help us meditate on the barrier until it reveals the deeper hurt, pain, or fear that is generating it, which is often connected to earlier, unhealed memories. We need to recognize Jesus' experience of this same type of hurt and allow him to be with us in the midst of our pain. We need to offer our willingness to be healed in a way which honors both the reality of our suffering and the new possibilities we now have to relate to others and to the world around us (*Lectionary Homiletics,* May 1994, p. 3f.). When the barriers to love have been removed we can now carry on with our own ministry of love, healing, and reconciliation as our text challenges us to do in verse 11.

Love Involves Risk

Because love involves risks many are willing to allow their definition of love to remain sentimental and abstract. When God so loved the world God took a risk. This risk could result in the rejection and death of God's son. This is exactly what happened. If God's love incarnate in Jesus cost him his life, it is inconceivable that a person living a Christ-like life would be without cost. Responding to the call of Christ can be a risky business. Jesus one day met an affluent young man who asked, "What must I do to inherit the kingdom of heaven?" Jesus responded, "Take what you have, sell it and give the money to the poor, and then come and follow me." The young man left because he felt the price was too high. There is a risk in asking such a question of Jesus. But the demand of the kingdom of God has never been any less. There is a risk in following Jesus — it can be a risk to your possessions, your ambitions, your values, even your expectations. The call of Christ has a way of totally upsetting and redirecting one's life. Ask the apostle Paul.

What about all of those who have suffered for the sake of love? There is a risk involved for those who love deeply. If you don't think so, then ask Oscar Romero, Dietrich Bonhoeffer, and Martin Luther King, Jr. If you don't think that love causes pain then ask Desmond Tutu and Nelson Mandela, along with the multitude who are unknown and unnamed who sought to love deeply and paid dearly. In Norman Maclean's *A River Runs Through It,* there is the example of love taking risks for the well-being of another when the elder brother Norman relentlessly responds to the needs of his difficult younger brother Paul through escalating bouts of drinking, fighting, and gambling. At his brother Paul's eventual death in a gambling brawl, Norman muses, "It is possible to love completely, without complete understanding." Norman's grieving father, a Presbyterian minister, responds, "That I have known and preached."

Love — Being Christ To Others

In the United Methodist *Book of Worship* I have had deep appreciation for the prayer at the end of the service of Word and Table which reads: "Grant that we may go into the world in the strength of your Spirit, to give ourselves for others, in the name of Jesus Christ our Lord, Amen."

After we share together the bread and the cup, celebrating that moment when God's love in Christ is made visible, then we depart from the table to go in the strength of the Spirit to give ourselves for others in the name of Christ. Now it is possible for the Word to be made visible through our lives as we serve others. Joan Delaplane, Professor of Pastoral Theology at Aquinas Institute of Theology, told what a dear friend had said to her as her friend was dying, "You are a sacrament of God's love for me." She said, "Isn't that what we are all called to be to one another — a sacrament of God's love?" We need to be for one another part of what Jesus is for us — one who heals, nourishes, strengthens, forgives, and challenges. It was Basil the Great who said, "The bread which you do not use is the bread of the hungry. The clothes hanging in your closet are the clothes for the naked. The shoes you do not wear are the shoes for the one who is barefoot. The money you keep locked away is the money of the poor." Maybe this is what Scott Peck had in mind when he wrote, "Call it what you will, genuine love, with all the discipline it requires, is the only path to substantial joy. The more I love, the longer I love, the larger I become. Genuine love is self-replenishing" (*The Road Less Traveled,* p. 28).

Shortly after he came to Park Avenue Presbyterian Church in New York City, David H. C. Read said he was speeding down Park Avenue in a taxi with D. T. Niles, the Methodist scholar and evangelist from Sri Lanka, taking him to catch his train at Grand Central Station. He said that they were involved in a vigorous debate regarding homiletics and the theology behind it. As Niles got out of the taxi, he stuck his head in the window. "David," he said, "in the end there is only one thing to say: God loves you. Good-bye!" He said a few days later he was on the edge of a huge crowd in Central Park and heard the familiar voice of Billy Graham on the loudspeaker, "God so loved the world ..." He said a few years earlier I might have been tempted to say, "Here we go again." Then he looked at the faces around him — young, teenage, adult, and old. In spite of all of the distractions the people were listening. Graham spoke of the contrast between his text and the city around them — crime, drugs, violence, cruelty — and the people listened. Read said in their faces he could read the question: "Is there really such a God?"

Yes! There is.

A Victorious Faith

1 John 5:1-6

The theme of the text is: anyone who believes Jesus is the Christ is born of God and by this faith overcomes the world. That's what we want today — a faith that gives us the victory to overcome the world. If there is one thing we want from our faith, it is the assurance that there is more to life than what we see on televison and read about in the newspapers. If this is all there is to life, then we are indeed most miserable. When public figures flout decency and morality, when trusted officials violate our trust, when a disregard for fidelity and integrity among spouses, families, and business leaders becomes commonplace, when we constantly see the lack of any kind of peace with justice and the poor, the marginal, and the weak are the constant victims of the strong and powerful, it is then that we seek a faith that will overcome the world. We seek a faith that tells us that right, goodness, honesty, decency, and fair play are still the essential qualities of human life, and they are the values that in the long run will prevail and they are still principles to live by when so many would say otherwise. We want a faith that tells us that there is more to life than the shallow, self-centered, egotistical lifestyles portrayed by so many entertainers and professional athletes. Their omnipresent images are constantly paraded before us by the media. They are not only depressing, but downright boring.

For we who live in this world, the author states that "this is the victory that conquers the world, our faith." He reminds us that this faith is centered in Jesus Christ and this faith is what renders a person a child of God (v. 5). It has been pointed out that a person can enter into a certain kind of faith other than belief in Christ. For instance, a philosopher can by his thought arrive at the conclusion that we live in a theistic world. An artist can know God as beauty. Many have come to the conclusion that God is moral. The text declares that only through God's self-revelation in Jesus can one comprehend how God loves the world and how our life in him is to be lived out in love. The writer of 1 John states that proof of whether one is a child of God is made evident by one's love for others, and a failure to love others would invalidate one's relationship with God. "When a person believes that Jesus is the Christ he enters into the distinctive solidarity of Christian fellowship" (Paul W. Hoon, *The Interpreter's Bible,* vol. 12, p. 289).

Our ethical and benevolent actions and deeds only become Christian when they are impelled by the prior love of God. A life of kind deeds and loving concern is good, but those that are inspired by the love of God are better. The story is told about children in a Chinese village who declined to accept needed medication offered them by a government station. Instead they walked several miles further to get the same medicine from a Christian missionary. When they were asked why they did so, they replied, "The medicine is the same, but the hands are different." Service motivated by the love of God makes a difference.

Overcoming The World

The declaration of the text is clear: "This is the victory that overcomes the world, our faith" (v. 4). For the author, the victory that overcomes the world matches at every point the assaults and temptations of the world. It is a victory of joy over unhappiness (1:1); of fellowship over loneliness (2:19); of honesty over pride and self-deception (1:6-10); of righteousness over sin (2:1-2, 12-13; 5:18); of love over hatred (2:10); of eternal life over time and death (1:2; 2:17; 5:11-13, 20). The point being that the battlefield on which the believer overcomes the world is not that of thought or theology, but the area of everyday living. It is the everyday struggles with the cares of life that the Christian faith either wins or loses. But the faith that prevails is centered in Christ. That is the content of this faith. It is not a belief in stoical courage, mere optimism that will automatically prevail. It is not a trust in luck, fate, faith in progress, or confidence in one's ability. It is faith in Jesus Christ as the Son of God — here we find the faith we are looking for defined in concrete, human terms in the life of Jesus. This faith lives itself out in the world in a manner expressed by Mother Teresa in her book, *Words to Love By*:

> *At the end of life we will not be judged by*
> *how many diplomas we have received,*
> *how much money we have made,*
> *how many great things we have done.*

> *We will be judged by*
> *"I was hungry and you gave me to eat,*
> *I was naked and you clothed me,*
> *I was homeless and you took me in."*

> *Hungry, not for bread,*
> *but hungry for love.*
> *Naked, not for clothing,*
> *but naked of human dignity and respect.*
> *Homeless, not only for want of a room of bricks,*
> *but homeless because of rejection.* (p. 77)

Overcoming The Pressures

The New Testament has another word for us when the apostle Paul said, "For whenever I am weak, I am strong" (2 Corinthians 12:10). He is saying that strength is brought to its completion in weakness. This is the strength that overcomes the world. It was for Paul a faith that was constantly put under pressure. It was in those moments when he felt inadequate and weak that faith was the victory that overcame weakness. Paul knew the pressure as we know the pressure. The pressures we face are real. We know the pressures of a demanding job. If you do not produce then somebody is nearby to replace you who will produce. We all know the pressures of difficult relationships. We know the pressures of living in a world community that has lost heart and faith, and we so desperately want to relate the message of the Gospel of Christ to this world. We know the pressures of living in a world of fear. As the American embassies were bombed in Kenya and Tanzania recently and the U.S. went on the offensive with the missile strikes in Afganistan and Sudan, we lived in fear — fear that we would be the victims of a terrorist attack. There is deep-seated fear in the land. How does our faith give us the victory over such fear? So many have fears that are difficult to deal with because they are the fears within. Those fears are there when you get up in the morning and when you try to go to sleep at night. They are the fears of doubt and listlessness causing depression, one of the most widespread fears of our time. We so desperately want to win this battle and be free again. These pressures are real; fear is real; depression and anxiety are real. But, the ever-living presence of Christ in the midst of our fears and pressures is also real. The faith that gives us the victory is a faith that believes that Christ was raised up in the first century as the victor over death and darkness and he has been raised up in all times and into our time. "Who is it that conquers the world but the one who believes that Jesus is the Son of God?" (v. 5).

The Faith That Keeps Us Going

A book that has meant much to me in my faith journey has been Frederick Buechner's *Longing for Home*. Buechner, who is now in his seventies, looks back with a candid and searching examination for the meaning, power, and importance of home in our lives. It is a deeply moving book of reflection and recollection. At the end of his book he talks about faith. For him doubt is not the opposite of faith, but an element of faith; in other words, doubt goes hand in hand with faith. There are those moments when all of our statements of faith seem to ring wrong. "There are times when it is hard to see how any honest, intelligent person can look at the world without concluding as Macbeth did that the whole show is a tale told by an idiot, full of sound and fury and signifying nothing" (p. 169). We have faith but at the same time we have doubts. But our doubts prove that we are in touch with reality, those things that both threaten faith as well as nourish it. If we are not in touch with reality, then our faith is apt to be blind, fragile, and irrelevant. He reminds us that if we have no doubts we are either kidding ourselves or asleep. His classic definition of doubt is: "Doubts are the ants in the pants of faith. They keep it awake and moving" (Buechner, *Wishful Thinking*, p. 20).

In seeking a faith that overcomes the world, how can we describe faith in a world of so much perpetual suffering? Our century is one of unprecedented suffering. It appears that God leaves people free to do unspeakable things to each other. But at the same time, if people are not truly free, they are not truly human as God intended them to be. To be humanly free means that people are free to do unspeakable things to each other, at the same time participating in the most loving and compassionate deeds of human kindness and love. The human freedom that God has endowed to each of us makes it possible to believe in God in spite of suffering. What about the suffering that does not involve human freedom, such as disease, disability, and natural disasters? As I am writing this sermon, I am listening to the news reports of Hurricane Bonnie which has winds of 120 miles per hour and a breadth of 200 miles and is just about to lash the coast of the Carolinas. Buechner reminds us that maybe the explanation for natural disaster is "that God leaves creation itself free either to run as it was created to run or to run amok, and that the doctrine of the Fall pertains not just to the human order but to the natural order as well. Maybe so, but maybe not so" (*Longing for Home*, p. 169). I have some doubts. Could it not be that the natural phenomena of tornadoes, hurricanes, and storms are part of God's initial created order, and we just happened to get in the way? These storms are destructive in regard to personal life and property, but they also have an awesome beauty all their own. I am aware, as Buechner is aware, that there are times when all of our explanations ring false even as we make them.

What about the future? What about tomorrow? Can we look with confidence to the days ahead which appear so dark, dreary, and threatening for so many? What word can we speak to those who feel like they are looking into an abyss which will help them not to feel devastated? How can we acquire that faith that helps us to overcome the world? The future appeared dismal in many ways to the apostle Paul, but I am convinced we can take courage from the words he spoke to the Corinthians: "For now we see in a mirror, dimly, but then we will see face to face. Now I know only in part; then I will know fully, even as I have been known" (1 Corinthians 13:12). It is the nature of faith to look beyond itself, beyond the doubts that will always exist on this side of time, until we experience life on the other side of time and we are able to see more clearly. I am reminded that in the meantime faith is the way we have of seeing while we have only the dark glass to see through.

Celebrating The Absence Of The Presence

Ephesians 1:15-23

We find it easy to celebrate Jesus' coming at Christmas, but Ascension Day goes by mostly unnoticed. Well, why not? How can we celebrate the absence of the presence? However, don't we do this every Sunday morning as we recite the creed, "He ascended into heaven?" After saying this all of these years, do we know what it means? It appears to us as a most incredible story, and it raises many questions. If we take the story literally as Luke does in Acts 1, what can we do with it in light of our modern knowledge of outer space? How is it that 2,000 years ago a group of men and women on a hilltop in Palestine watched one of their number take off vertically from the ground and disappear into a cloud, proceeding nonstop until he arrived at a precise location in space called heaven? There is no *up* and *down* in space. So where did Jesus go? You are probably saying to yourself, "How does this have any practical application for our faith today?" But Jesus spoke directly about his going. He said, "It is to your advantage that I go away, for if I do not go away, the Counselor (the Holy Spirit) will not come to you" (John 16:7). He went on to say that the Holy Spirit would teach believers all things. He would bring to remembrance all that Jesus had said. He would guide believers into all truth.

The Ascension Affirms The Presence Of Christ

In essence Jesus is saying there is a new divine presence coming into the world, the Holy Spirit, who is even more real and powerful than was his earthly ministry. The time of the historical Jesus must end, and so it does, so that the new age of the Spirit may

95

begin. What does the Ascension of Jesus mean to us? First, the Ascension affirms that the presence of Christ was not limited to the first century, but is for all centuries, all times, and all places. Christ is now a living presence among us. He comes to our age, to every being, and to us. Christ is present here and now.

What happened in Palestine in the first century has eternal dimensions. It reaches right here to the heart of every problem, to every life. In the first century Jesus walked the shores of Galilee; today Jesus walks the streets of our cities. In the first century he healed the blind, the lame, and the leper. Today he comes to every hospital room and bedside among the sick and dying with the comfort of his presence. In the first century he entered the home of Mary and Martha; today he wants to enter your home. He met Nicodemus at night and counseled with him over a troubling problem. Today he seeks to come to you amid those agonizingly long, dark hours of night to assist you with those perplexing problems that keep you from rest and sleep. In the first century Jesus quieted the tempest on the Sea of Galilee. Today he seeks to quiet the tempest in your soul, mind, and heart. In the first century, Jesus looked out over the city and said: "O Jerusalem, Jerusalem, the city that murders the prophets and stones the messengers sent to her! How often have I longed to gather your children, as a hen gathers her brood under her wings; but you would not let me" (Matthew 23:37 NEB).

Today, Jesus looks out over our broken, polluted, divided, and violent world and says to us, "You who have killed the prophets, ravished the earth, and polluted its atmosphere; you who have created such a violent earth of killing, stealing, and plundering, where the strong victimize the weak; you who build bombs and missiles capable of destroying yourselves many times over! How often have I wanted to gather you as my children under my wings, as a hen would gather her chicks, but you would not let me."

What God did in Jesus' day in Palestine, God continues to do through the Holy Spirit today.

96

The Lordship Of Christ

Second, the Ascension is a clear statement about the lordship of Christ. The one who was struck down and humiliated, but who has been raised and is now ascended and returned to God triumphant — he is given power and authority, and to him every knee shall bow.

To say the ascended Christ is the Lord of the earth is the most political statement that the Church can make. For this statement declares that no king, no head of state, no president, prime minister, or dictator is the greatest — each one comes under the rule and reign of Christ who is the Lord of lords and the King of kings. "Therefore God raised him up to the heights and bestowed on him the name above all names, that at the name of Jesus every knee should bow — in heaven, on earth, and in the depths — and every tongue confess, 'Jesus Christ is Lord,' to the glory of God the Father" (Philippians 2:10-11 NEB).

Do you realize the magnitude of this statement? It means that all in authority or who have power or influence, those in charge of vast multinational companies, those who control economies and who manage the great institutions of the world are all answerable to the ascended Christ. It means that those who bring about war, those whose business is terror are answerable to the ascended Lord.

The lordship of Christ means that he claims the life of the world as his own. The life of Christ should be reflected in the world in all of our human relations. It should be evident in the way we help the poor, feed the hungry, and seek to liberate the oppressed without any ulterior motive but simply to be faithful to Christ who is the Lord of all. Although many in the world lack awareness of Christ's claim upon them, this should not divert us from the central truth of the Ascension — that Jesus Christ, the Lord of all, has cosmic reign over both heaven and earth.

What does it mean for individuals like you and me to say that Jesus Christ is Lord? It means that we acknowledge his word and accept him as the Lord of life. To say that Christ is the Lord means that we are willing to surrender our freedom and live under Christ's rule. To confess that Jesus Christ is Lord is to affirm that in all things he has priority. We acknowledge the lordship of Christ by

97

making his ways primary in our lives. We love one another, not because it makes us feel good, but because it is the way of Christ who in love gave his life for us.

God Is In Control

Third, the Ascension affirms for us that God is in control. All the obstacles are overcome and Christ is resurrected and has ascended to the Father. He is Lord of all. He is King forever and God is in control. The pessimism, despair, and frustration that is evident in the life of the Church stems from our doubt about whether God is really in control. Would there not be a greater sense of optimism and hope and a greater willingness to take risks if we really believed that God was in control? The early apostles put their lives on the line. They were willing to risk everything. Why? Because they were convinced of the lordship of Christ and they had no doubt that God was in control. The apostle Paul points out that Christ "must reign until he puts all his enemies under his feet. The last enemy to be destroyed is death" (1 Corinthians 15:25-26).

God is in control! George MacDonald, during a troubled period of his life, said, "All of his windows were darkened, except the skylight." He went on to say that not all of his problems were solved. There were many nagging questions that were still unsettled. But he was convinced that as long as he had God that was all that mattered. We don't need to wait until we can explain the universe or give satisfactory answers in terms of logic and theory to its baffling enigmas. It is not an explanation or a theory that we need; it is the reinforcing presence of Christ, and if we have that we can march on without waiting or without fear.

The apostle was so certain that God was in control that he could say, "in everything God works for good with those who love him, who are called according to his purpose" (Romans 8:28). Do you see what this means for you and me? Can you say that? I must admit that there are times I do not see that happening. There are some things, especially suffering and death, that just do not seem to fit into any scheme or pattern. But the apostle is saying that with God in charge there can be no irreparable disaster, no deep ills that cannot yield overwhelming good, no thorns that cannot be woven into a crown.

If God is in control then what are we waiting for? Can we make that leap of faith fully trusting in the love of God? Can we live boldly and recklessly, casting ourselves with confidence upon the love and care of God and trusting wholly in God's grace? When I was in college I had a Greek professor who tried to impress on our minds that the orignal meaning of the word *faith* involved commitment. He told us the story about a man who came to a town who had the reputation of being the world's greatest tightrope walker. On the edge of town was a deep gorge. The man suspended a delicate wire across the gorge and invited the entire town to come out and watch him cross over the gorge on the wire. His custom was to use a wheelbarrow to balance himself as he walked across the wire. Just before he was to start across the gorge he asked the man standing next to him, "Do you think that I can do it?" The man, knowing about his reputation, said without hesitation, "Yes." He said to him, "Then you get in the wheelbarrow." The question is: Do you believe all these things the Bible says about Jesus? Do you believe that he is the ascended Lord, the King of kings, the Lord of lords, the Son of God? If so, are you willing to commit your life to him?

As far as the Ascension is concerned, Jesus was never more present than when he was absent. Jesus, in a sense, did not go away, but because of the coming of the Holy Spirit, where he once dwelt *among* the people, he now dwells *within* them.

Life — And Then Some

1 John 5:9-13

The words of the text express clearly the central theme of 1 John. The author has dealt with many themes, and his mind has wandered in several directions. But he has always kept his main theme in mind, which he now states clearly in these closing verses: "Whoever has the Son has life." He states unequivocally that his overall purpose for his writing is "that you may know that you have eternal life." There is no doubt that 1 John through the centuries has nourished souls, kindled faith, and inspired love. Keeping these thoughts in mind, let us pursue the subject a bit further.

Life Is God's Gift

To be a live human being, to breathe, to think, simply to be, is a glorious thing. Walter J. Burghardt in his book *Preaching the Just Word* says that life is glorious because it is a gift. Not merely a gift from our parents, life is a gift "from above." It is a gift from God who gives all that is good, as James reminds us in 1:17: "Every generous act of giving, with every perfect gift, is from above, coming down from the Father of lights, with whom there is no variation or shadow due to change." The gift of life is a sharing in God who is *life*.

Human life is a glorious gift because it is a gift of love. Burghardt has pointed out that God has not just fashioned you to be, but you are a special kind of existence. You share "being" with stone and star, with sea and sand. You share a form of life with winter wheat and quivering aspen leaf. Along with robins, lions, and dolphins you can see and hear and touch and taste and smell.

> *But what makes you human is a twin power you alone
> of earth's creatures share with God. Whatever your
> blood, skin, or accent, male or female, you come into
> this world sharing two of God's precious perfections:
> You have the power to know, and you have the freedom
> to love. You are someone; you are a person; you are
> like God* (Burghardt, p. 27).

Thus, life is good because it is from God. All that God creates and gives is good.

Life With A Purpose

Archdeacon Paley argued that if you examine the intricate mechanism of a watch, you cannot fail to believe that it has been produced by a purposeful agent, namely, a watchmaker. He went on to reason that by analogy when one reflects on the world with all of its wealth of natural resources, beauty, and orderliness one cannot help but to conclude that there must be a world-maker, a creator God. The glaring weakness in Paley's argument is that God is not only transcendent, but immanent. The God who is revealed in the struggle with the Hebrew people in their nomadic trek from slavery to freedom, the God revealed in the life of Jesus Christ is a God of immanent feeling and identification with all that God created. God is not only over creation but God is within it. The biblical narrative strongly presents a God who became incarnate in the midst of life, that in Christ the Word became in-fleshed in history and suffered in history and the Holy Spirit still groans in travail with the world, seeking to bring to birth the children of God. As one scholar has pointed out, "The purpose of God for the world is not realized by some effortless decree issuing from the heavenly places, but demands God's presence and God's very self in the midst of the world" (John Macquarrie, *Christian Hope,* p. 83).

All of us have some purpose for what we do and how we live. But we need to have a main purpose, a central, all-consuming purpose that holds life together when other things begin to erode and fade away. Tillich called this main purpose an "ultimate concern" which embraces and coordinates all the little purposes. Can we believe that God has a purpose for the whole creation, a purpose that gathers up, purifies, and deepens all our finite purposes? Jesus believed that there was such a purpose. He called it the Kingdom of God. Within the life and teachings of Christ we discover the nature, the purpose, the meaning, and the demands of this Kingdom upon our lives. The purpose of the Christian life is to seek first the Kingdom of God. This brings direction, purpose, and meaning to life.

> *If the creator was no more than a "pure mathematician," as Sir James Jeans once described God, then God might have been content with a universe of galaxies and stars and planets, of physics and chemistry intricately ordered, and that would certainly be a universe to fill our minds with awe. But God, Christians believe, is more than a pure mathematician, the universe is more than a machine, more than an overwhelming esthetic creation. God is a God of love, whose purpose in creation was not to bring into being a fascinatingly beautiful universe, but to be confronted with an "other" who could respond to love with love, who could live communion.* — Macquarrie, *ibid.*

So life emerges in creation. This life has direction and purpose. In the life of Christ we can then begin to understand God's purpose for creation. This is uniquely expressed in Jesus' teaching and preaching regarding the kingdom of God. The more we become Christ-like, the more we become part of the kingdom, the more our life acquires meaning and purpose. "I have come that they may have life, and have it more abundantly" (John 10:10b).

Life Finds Purpose In Community

In our text the author declares, "Whoever has the Son has life." The author is not speaking as a voice in the wilderness, isolated and alone. He is speaking as a member of the first century Christian community. It is from within this community that he has gained such insight to life, and it is this community that has nurtured this

103

new life in Christ, and it is this community that empowers him to make such a proclamation. The claim of the New Testament writers is that this community of faith is where the new believer is welcomed, accepted, trained, nurtured, and saved. These new human communities have been described by scholars not as escapists but rather as fragile societies organized in response to the Jesus event, who were trying to provide a home for widows, aliens, immigrants, displaced workers, the poor, and others who were in need. They were multilingual and multicultural creations of a new humanity who sought the power of healing, love, and justice. Keith Russell has pointed out that the early church rejected the culture of privilege and power.

> *The emerging church was not a subset of the dominant culture. Its dramatic growth did not come about because it was favored or protected by the state. It was not a tax-exempt, not-for-profit organization. It was a sect existing on the edge of the Roman society, often outside societal laws and mores or at least substantially at odds with them ... The early church grew rapidly in part because, like other sects, it offered its adherents love and acceptance within the community; that is, the church became a primary place of belonging in urban areas in time of severe social dislocation. The church provided a welcoming home and a place of acceptance for aliens, exiles, and displaced people all over the Roman Empire. It was a new family, a new community that claimed a new unity in response to Christ.*
> — *The Living Pulpit,* July-September 1995, p. 10

As then, so now, conversion to Christ is a concession to the community of faith — the Church. One's acceptance of Christ and admission into the community is attested to by public baptism. Baptism is a public confession of Jesus Christ as Lord and a declaration that one has now decided to become a member of this community called the Church. This act of confession, repentance, and baptism promises a new sense of self and a new sense of purpose. That is, it provides new life.

Choose Life

The text declares that by choosing Christ one has chosen life. One theme that the author of 1 John has consistently followed is that the abundant life that Jesus offers, which is life born of the spirit of God, is life in which the love of God is expressed in love for other human beings. "Whoever does not love does not know God, for God is love" (4:8). "... if we love one another, God lives in us, and his love is perfected in us" (4:12b). "Little children, let us love, not in word and speech, but in truth and action" (3:18). By choosing Christ we have accepted an ethic of love, and now our judgments of one another in regard to what is right and wrong can be spoken by seeing God in one's neighbor. Jesus told Nicodemus that the second birth is not from flesh and blood, but from the Spirit. It is also true that those born of God's spirit are born into love and respect for human life. This is the central message of 1 John — the author is emphatic that "whoever does not love does not know God, for God is love" (4:8b). Again he states, "The commandment we have from him is this: those who love God must love their brothers and sisters also" (4:21). To choose life is to choose compassion, justice, healing, but above all — love.

Books In This Cycle B Series

GOSPEL SET
A God For This World
Sermons for Advent/Christmas/Epiphany
Maurice A. Fetty

The Culture Of Disbelief
Sermons For Lent/Easter
Donna E. Schaper

The Advocate
Sermons For Sundays After Pentecost (First Third)
Ron Lavin

Surviving In A Cordless World
Sermons For Sundays After Pentecost (Middle Third)
Lawrence H. Craig

Against The Grain — Words For A Politically Incorrect Church
Sermons For Sundays After Pentecost (Last Third)
Steven E. Albertin

FIRST LESSON SET
Defining Moments
Sermons For Advent/Christmas/Epiphany
William L. Self

From This Day Forward
Sermons For Lent/Easter
Paul W. Kummer

Out From The Ordinary
Sermons For Sundays After Pentecost (First Third)
Gary L. Carver

Wearing The Wind
Sermons For Sundays After Pentecost (Middle Third)
Stephen M. Crotts

Out Of The Whirlwind
Sermons For Sundays After Pentecost (Last Third)
John A. Stroman

SECOND LESSON SET
Humming Till The Music Returns
Sermons For Advent/Christmas/Epiphany
Wayne Brouwer

Ashes To Ascension
Sermons For Lent/Easter
John A. Stroman